WORLD CONCE[RNS]

W. E. Marsden
Department of Education, University of Liverpool

V. M. Marsden
Greenbank High School, Southport

Oliver & Boyd

Acknowledgements

The publishers would like to thank the following for permission to reproduce photographs and other copyright material:

Barnaby's Picture Library (1.2, 1.3, 1.20, 2.6, 3.4, 3.23, 4.7, 5.5, 6.1, 6.2, 6.3, 6.16, 6.17, 6.19); Photosource (1.4, 1.5, 5.2, 5.6, 5.9); Christian Aid (1.7, 1.13, 2.1, 3.1, 3.2, 3.9, 3.14, Murray 3.22, 4.2, 4.3, 4.4, 4.14, 4.15, 6.14, 6.15, 7.1, 7.13); World Bank (1.12 Within, 1.14 Sennett, 3.16 Sennett, 3.17 Within, 3.19 Hadar, 3.20 Within, 4.9 Chernush, 4.16 Within, 7.2 Hadar, 7.11); Mansell (1.17, 4.19, 6.8, 6.18); United Nations (1.18, 8.7); Christine Osborne (1.19, 7.16); Times Newspapers Limited (2.4, 8.12); S Ferguson (2.5, 3.10, 3.11); Syndication International (2.7 J Barr); Marion and Tony Morrison (2.9, 2.10, 2.11, 2.13, 2.14, 6.20, 7.8, 7.9, 7.12, 8.6); Centre for World Development Education (2.12 P. Crooke); Oxfam (3.15); Popperfoto (3.24, 7.10); British Library from 1883 *Illustrated London News* vol. 83 no. 2316 (4.6); UNICEF (4.11); Save the Children Fund (4.17 Wells); ZEFA (5.7, 6.5, 7.4, 7.15); J Allan Cash (5.11, 6.4, 6.6, 6.23, 8.2); W E Marsden (6.9, 6.10, 6.11); US Air Force (6.12); Frank Spooner (6.22, 8.5, 8.10, 8.13, 8.14, 8.15); Hutchison Library (6.24); Gerald Cubitt (6.25); International Planned Parenthood Federation (7.3); Richard Willson (7.6); Picturepoint (8.3); Rex Features (8.11).

The cover photographs show forest clearance, Ecuador (Picturepoint), Aberdeen, Hong Kong (Photosource) and Cyclone David (John Hillelson).

The title page photograph shows a bus stuck in the mud, Brazil (Popperfoto).

The authors wish to acknowledge the following sources which were used as a basis for figures.
World Development Report, World Bank 1981 (3.3); East Midlands Examining Board, Syllabus 2, Paper 1, 1982 (3.8); *Earthwatch* No. 11, 1982, p.7/original source Jacques Bugnicourt, ENDA (7.5); *People* vol. 10, no. 4, 1983 (7.14); Oxfam (8.8); Save the Children Fund (8.9).

Oliver & Boyd
Robert Stevenson House
1-3 Baxter's Place
Leith Walk
Edinburgh EH1 3BB
A division of Longman Group UK Ltd

First published 1986

© Oliver & Boyd 1986. All rights reserved. No part of this publication may be reproduced, stored in a retrieval system, or transmitted in any form or by any means, electronic, mechanical, photocopying, recording or otherwise, without the prior written permission of the publishers.

Typesetting, design and artwork by Swanston Graphics, Derby, England

Typeface Bembo Light 12/13

**Produced by Longman Group (FE) Ltd
Printed in Hong Kong**

ISBN 0-05-003843-5

Contents

1	**World population**	**4**
	Population distribution and density	4
	World population growth	7
	The demographic transition	8
	Age structure	8
	High population growth: India	9
	People on the move: migration	10
2	**Urbanisation**	**13**
	The world's 'million cities'	13
	Problems of urbanisation	14
	The shanty towns of South America	16
	Advantages of urbanisation	18
3	**Rich and poor worlds**	**19**
	Developed and developing countries	19
	Measuring rich and poor	21
	Food supply	22
	Health	24
	Education	28
4	**Natural disasters**	**29**
	Earthquakes: Peru	29
	Volcanoes: two Indonesian Islands	30
	Cyclones and floods: Bangladesh	31
	Drought: the Sahel	33
	Insect pests	34
5	**Tourism in the developing world: the Caribbean**	**36**
	The growth of international tourism	36
	Advantages of tourism to the islands	39
	Problems brought by tourism	40
6	**Human conflict**	**41**
	Religious difference	41
	Language difference	42
	Political difference	43
	Ethnic (racial) difference	46
7	**Environmental concern**	**51**
	Agricultural land	51
	Water supplies	52
	Forests	53
	Wildlife	56
8	**Interdependence**	**57**
	North and South	57
	Lack of cooperation: unequal terms of trade	58
	Cooperation: international aid	60
	Index	64

1 World population

Population distribution and density

One of the most difficult problems facing the world today is rapid population growth. This can lead to too many people being crowded into small areas. Not all countries are experiencing this, however. The **population distribution** over the earth varies a great deal. Distribution refers to the way people are spread out over an area of land. 1.1 is a map showing by dots the distribution of people in the Americas and East Asia/Australasia. Each dot represents a certain number of people. In some areas there are few dots to be seen. Here the population is widely spread out, or **sparse**. In other areas the dots are so close together that they form a solid mass. In such areas the population is **dense**.

The **density of population** is the *ratio* of the number of people in an area to the amount of space in the area. It is usually expressed as *numbers of people per square kilometre*. For example, the most densely populated areas have over 200 people per square kilometre. The most sparsely peopled areas have less than 1 person per square kilometre.

Photographs 1.2, 1.3, 1.4 and 1.5 illustrate some landscapes typical of different population densities. 1.2 shows the steep, rocky, snow-capped slopes of the Andes mountains in south-west Argentina, where very few people live. In the rocky desert of Iran, shown on 1.3, water is in short supply and conditions are unpleasantly hot, so very few people live there. 1.4 is a photograph of part of Hong Kong. Here steep slopes have prevented the city from extending, so the vast population has been forced to live in high-rise apartments and even house boats. 1.5 shows terraced rice (padi) fields and plantations in Indonesia. The rural population is so dense here that even steep slopes must be farmed.

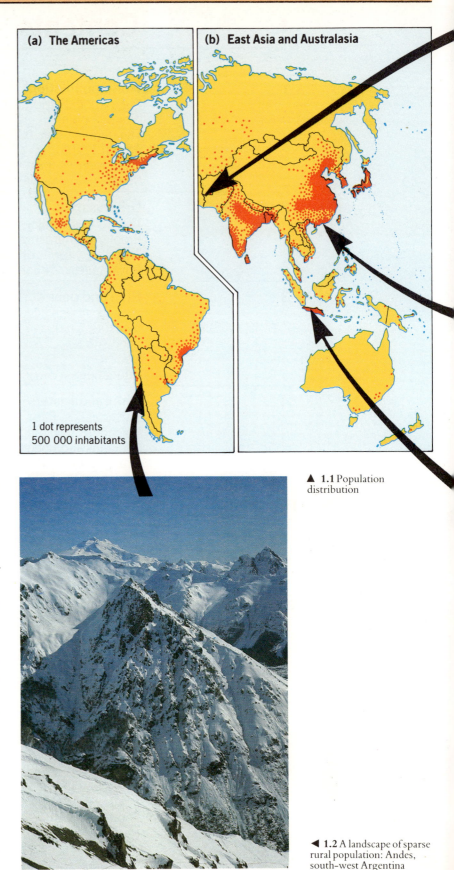

▲ 1.1 Population distribution

◀ 1.2 A landscape of sparse rural population: Andes, south-west Argentina

▲ 1.3 A landscape of sparse rural population: Iranian desert

▲ 1.4 A landscape of dense urban population: boat and high-rise living, Hong Kong

◄ 1.5 A landscape of dense rural population: rice paddies, Indonesia

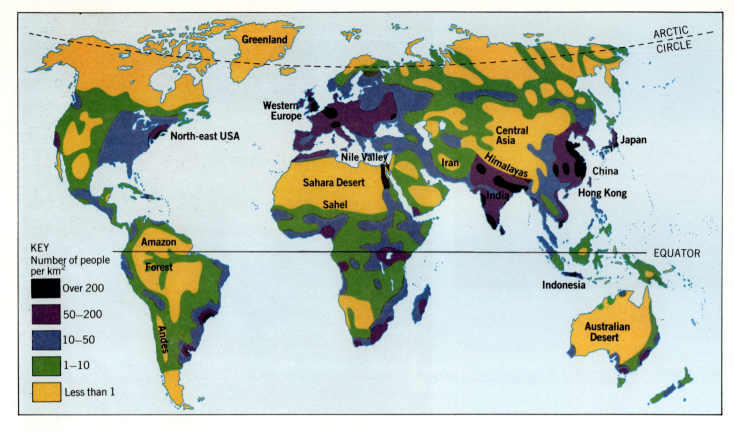

▲ 1.6 World population density

The different population densities over the whole world are shown on map 1.6. The **most densely populated areas** include those with

- **low-lying land**, for example, river valleys and coastal plains;
- **climates** which are warm enough and wet enough for crops to grow well;
- **thick fertile soils** which are rich in organic matter and easy to cultivate, such as the alluvial soils of river valleys;
- **ease of access**, both by land and water, again as in river valleys and flat coastal plains;
- **rich economic resources**, such as coalfields.

These conditions are to be found in different combinations in:

(a) the **Western (Occidental) world**, in Western Europe and north-eastern USA;

(b) the **Eastern (Oriental) world**, in India, China, Japan and Indonesia.

The **most sparsely populated areas** include those with

- **high land**, with bare rock and ice, steep slopes and sharp peaks, as in the Andean and Himalayan mountains, where population is concentrated in the valleys;
- **extreme climates**, whether very cold, as in Greenland, or very dry (and hot) as in the Sahara and Australian deserts;
- **thin, rocky or waterlogged soils**;
- **thick unbroken vegetation** such as the equatorial forest of Amazonia in South America;
- **poor access** to the coast, as in Central Asia;
- **few economic resources**, such as the Sahel countries of Africa.

These environments are sometimes called **hostile** by people of Western countries, most of whom live in towns. But the peoples who live in these areas have often adapted themselves very skilfully to the harsh conditions. They would no doubt find in turn that the crowds, traffic noise and pollution of urban areas in both Western and Eastern worlds were just as hostile.

World population growth

1.7 is a graph of world population growth since 1920, and projected to the year 2000. It is placed over a photograph of some of the huge population of Delhi, capital of India and one of the world's many fast-growing cities. As the graph shows, by 1940 the world's population had passed the *2 billion (2000 million)* mark, and by 1984 it had reached over *4½ billion*. At present rates of increase, it could be nearly 8 billion by the year 2000. (In 1982 alone, the world gained 80 million extra mouths to feed.) The 8 billion figure will not be reached, however, if the birth rate falls a lot. Later in this book we shall look at attempts being made to control it.

During the 1800s industrial Western countries such as Britain had a rapid growth in population. Since 1900, population growth has slowed down greatly in such countries. But it has increased tremendously in the so-called **developing countries** of the world: the poorer nations of Asia, Africa and Latin America.

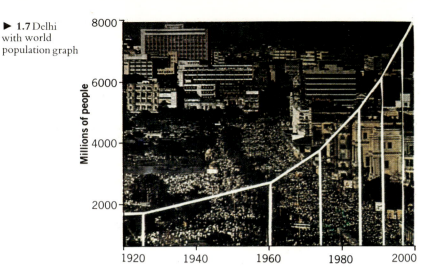

▶ 1.7 Delhi with world population graph

Map 1.8 shows population growth rates of over 2% in almost all of:

- **Latin America** north of Argentina, with 3% in countries such as Panama, Ecuador and Venezuela;
- **Africa**, with over 3% in countries such as Algeria, Libya, Ivory Coast, Kenya and Zimbabwe;
- **the Middle East**, with over 3% in, for example, Syria and Iraq;
- **South-east Asia**, with over 3% in Pakistan.

▼ 1.8 World population growth rates, 1984, by country

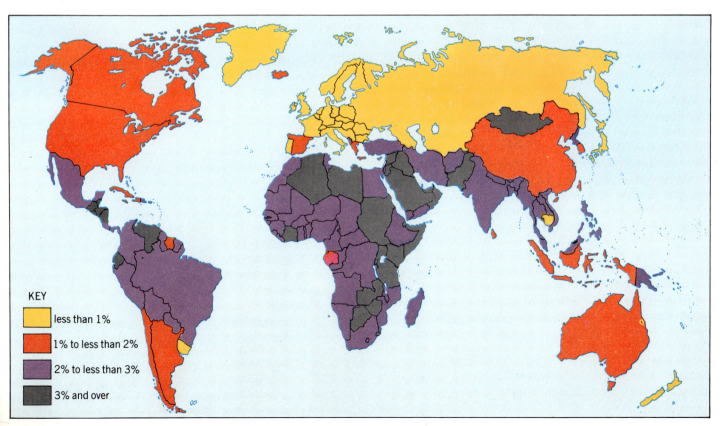

An annual growth rate of 3% means that a country of 100 million people would have 3 million more to feed each year, or 30 million over ten years.

By contrast, annual rates of less than 1% were to be found in the **developed countries** of the USA, most of Western Europe, and the 'communist world' of Eastern Europe and the USSR.

The demographic transition

1.9 shows that population growth depends on the balance between the birth rate and the death rate. If the birth rate is higher than the death rate, then the overall population grows. If they balance, the population remains steady.

Over the years population change has tended to pass through a series of stages (1.9). This is known as the **demographic transition**. It is marked by four different stages. Countries of the Western world, such as England and Wales, are at a later stage in the transition than those of the developing world.

Stage 1: Birth and death rates *fluctuate*, at a *high level*, but there is an overall balance and **population growth is small**. England and Wales were at this stage before 1750, and the developing world was at this stage before about 1950.

Stage 2: Birth rates remain high, at about 35 per thousand (and rising even to 40), but the death rate declines steadily from 30 to just over 20 per thousand population. In the early part of stage 2, **population growth is especially rapid**. This stage was experienced in England and Wales between 1750 and about 1875. The developing world is in stage 2 at the moment. The question is whether it can move quickly into stage 3 through control of the birth rate (see later).

Stage 3: Birth rates decline, from 35 to 20 per thousand, and death rates continue to fall. The birth rate remains higher than the death rate and **population growth continues**, but at a slower rate.

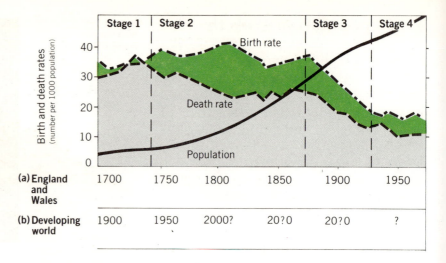

Stage 4: Birth and death rates *fluctuate*, at a *low level*, and **population growth is small**. The birth rate in England and Wales has come down to about 16 per thousand and the death rate to about 12 per thousand, in recent times. The developing world is far from reaching this stage. Most of it has not yet reached stage 3. It is difficult to judge what the future timing will be.

▲ 1.9 The demographic transition

Age structure

The **age structure** of a population also varies over the world and at different stages in the demographic transition. Comparing Western Europe and South America (1.10) we notice that South American countries have far more young people and far fewer old people in the population than Western European countries. This is to be expected

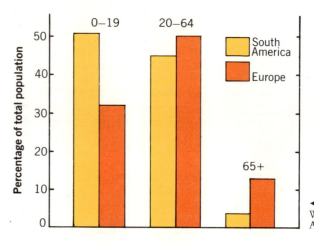

◀ 1.10 Age distribution: Western Europe and South America

since most South American countries are in stage 2 of the demographic transition (1.9). High birth rates give a large proportion of young people in the population, and high death rates give a small proportion of old people.

The more detailed bar graphs of 1.11 are presented horizontally to form a **population pyramid**. The broad base of the left hand side is typical of a developing country in stage 2 of the demographic transition. The right hand side is typical of a developed country in stage 4 of the transition, with a relatively large number of old people and small number of young people.

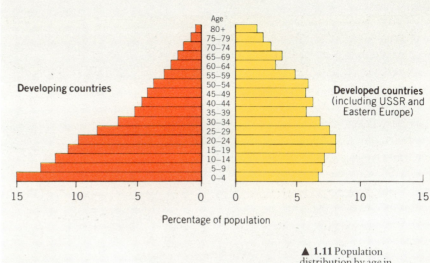

▲ 1.11 Population distribution by age in developing and developed countries

High population growth: India

1.12, 1.13 and 1.14 are pictures which illustrate what it can be like living under conditions of high population density, in countries such as India and Bangladesh. Map 1.15 shows that population densities in India vary, and are highest in the urban regions, for example round Calcutta, Delhi, Madras and Bombay. As 1.8 showed, India's population grows by over 2% each year. For an already huge population of over 650 million this growth rate is frighteningly high. Compare it, for example, with that of England and Wales: 0.1% in a population of 55 million.

◀ 1.13 Street living in Calcutta   ▲ 1.12 Crowds in Calcutta

▼ 1.14 Rail travel in Bangladesh

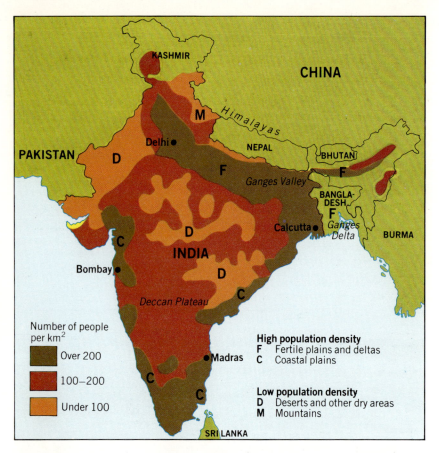

▲ 1.15 India: population density

Reasons for the high growth rate

Parents feel they must have large families for the following reasons.

- Many children still die young.
- Tradition encourages them to want boys more than girls, so those with girls continue to have more children.
- Children can help with work in the fields and at home.
- Children will support their parents when they are too old to work: there are no old-age pensions in India.

There is therefore resistance to family planning methods. Also,

- Medical improvements mean more people are surviving into old age.

Problems caused by the high growth rate

- A drift of people to the towns, increasing levels of unemployment.
- Severe overcrowding in villages and towns with many forced to live on the street (1.13).
- Poor hygiene and disease as a result of overcrowding and, where there is poverty and lack of food, malnutrition.
- Increasing numbers of children put a great strain on the educational system.

Possible improvements must include:

1. better farming practices to provide more food;
2. better medical care to improve health;
3. birth control programmes to limit families.

People on the move: migration

In any particular area, population change can result from the movement of people in or out of that area. Population movement is known as **migration**. **Immigration** is movement into an area, causing an increase in the population. **Emigration** is movement out of an area, causing a decrease in the population.

Migration is a complicated process, which takes place on different time scales.

1. Daily, for example,

(a) commuting from home to office;

(b) in some rural areas, from farmhouse or hut to distant pastures.

2. Seasonal, for example,

(a) nomads moving with the seasons in search of pastures;

(b) pilgrims journeying to holy cities at particular times of the year.

3. Semi-permanent, such as **migrant labour**, moving from one country to another in search of work, but intending to go back home eventually.

4. Permanent, that is, migration for life. It can be

(a) **voluntary migration**, where people move of their own choice; or

(b) **forced migration**, where people are compelled to move by some other group.

Voluntary migration

This is a result of two sets of factors, often working together to encourage people to move:
- **push factors**, persuading them to move away from their place of origin;
- **pull factors**, beckoning them to come to live in a new area.

Push factors are often a matter of necessity rather than free choice. Many people have migrated in the past to escape from poverty and famine: for example, the Irish in the early 1800s. But European peoples were also encouraged to emigrate during this period. One reason was to seek employment in the 'new worlds' of North America and Australia (1.16). Another reason was linked with the process of **colonisation** (where people from one country settle in and take control of another country or area). This began in the 1500s, but expanded greatly in the 1800s, by which time the whole of the Americas, Africa and Australasia had been colonised, mostly by European settlers (1.17).

During recent times, a reverse process has happened. In the late 1950s and early 1960s, for example, immigrants from 'New Commonwealth' countries such as the West Indies and India were encouraged to come to Britain to fill jobs. They were 'pushed out' from their homelands by poverty and unemployment. Similarly, people from south-east Europe have moved into Western Europe in search of work.

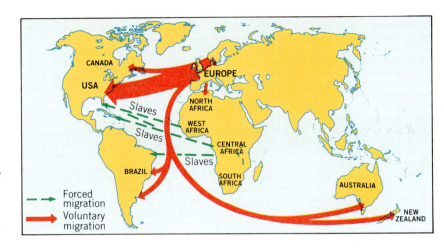

▲ 1.16 European emigration, 1800-1950, and the slave trade, 1700s

Forced migration

This is when people are driven out of their country by force, or under the threat of force, by ruthless governments or by opposing groups within the country. It might be because of their race, religion, customs, language, or for commercial greed or political reasons. Sometimes people have been forced to move to other areas and made to work.

▶ 1.17 Breakfast time on an emigrant ship, 1884

▲ **1.18** Palestinian emergency camp in Jordan, 1967

▲ **1.19** Palestinian refugee settlement in Jordan

◀ **1.20** Vietnamese boat people arriving in Hong Kong, 1980

Two examples are the **slave trade** (see 6.18) and the use of **prisoners of war** or **political prisoners**.

Refugees are people forced to move as a result of religious, political or racial persecution; or as a result of international or civil war and its aftermath. The most obvious example this century has been the Jews who fled from Europe because of persecution under Nazi-controlled governments. Of the 5.5 million Jews in Europe in the early 1900s, no more than 1.25 million were left in 1945. Millions had been murdered, and thousands of those who survived had fled. At the end of the Second World War, many of the Jews who were still in Europe also decided to leave. Most of them went to Palestine, which later became the Jewish state of Israel. This in turn forced a movement of other people, the Palestinian Arabs, who found themselves without a country of their own. Refugee camps were set up for the homeless. 1.18 shows a temporary camp in Jordan in 1967. 1.19 shows a more permanent refugee settlement in Jordan.

The Vietnamese civil war, which lasted for thirty years, created large numbers of refugees (as well as an enormous loss of life). It ended in the victory of the communist forces, who took over the government of the whole of Vietnam. This led more refugees to flee the country, including the 'boat people' who left by sea. Many were drowned but some reached safety, such as the group shown in 1.20, who found new homes in Hong Kong.

2 Urbanisation

▲ 2.1 Hong Kong: old and new housing

The world's 'million cities'

2.1 is a photograph of part of one of the world's **'million cities'**: Hong Kong (population 3½ million). Built on a site with little flat land, its densely packed buildings climb steep slopes. In 2.1 buildings from two periods of **urbanisation** can be seen: old tenements and new concrete tower blocks. A large proportion of Hong Kong's population lives in tiny flats in these tower blocks.

During the 1800s and early 1900s the world's most urbanised areas were Western Europe and north-eastern USA (2.2). But the developing countries have been catching up rapidly in the urbanisation process. 2.3 shows that developing countries now have more urban people than developed countries. Note, however, that most of the developing world's people are still rural.

The most interesting feature of urbanisation is the concentration of population in *large* towns and cities, and often in 'million cities'. 2.2 shows that these are now to be found in many parts of the developing world. Mexico City has over 14 million inhabitants, which makes it one of the world's largest. The newspaper extract (2.4) gives some idea of the frightening problems which arise when cities expand so quickly that local services are unable to cope. Mexico City's air pollution is made worse because the city is located in a mountain basin. The smog collects in the valley and tends to build up.

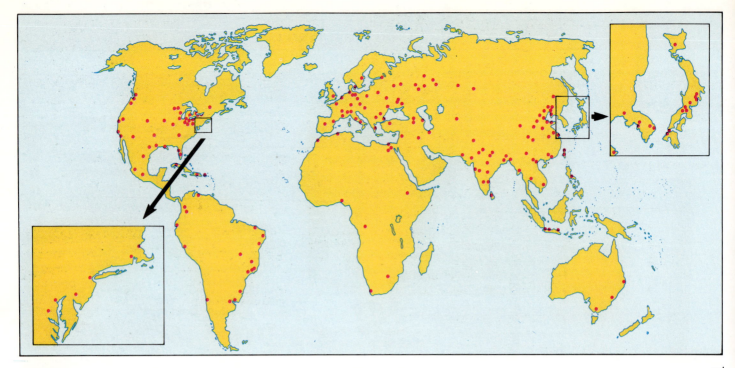

▲ 2.2 'Million cities': world cities of over one million population

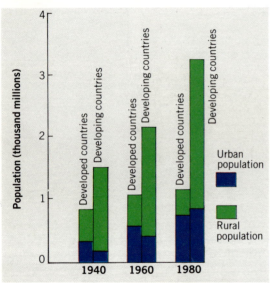

◀ 2.3 Changing urban and rural populations in developed and developing countries

> **I**n 1985 **Mexico City** will overtake Tokyo as the world's largest city, with more than 18m inhabitants. The city produces 6,000 more tons of rubbish daily than it can collect. It is so polluted that the effect of breathing its air for a day is as bad as smoking 40 cigarettes.
>
> With its outskirts ringed by nine giant shanty-towns, it is an apocalyptic image of a future, as close as the year 2000 ... By then, Mexico-City will have added nearly twice the current population of Greater London to its sprawling megalopolis.
>
> (*The Sunday Times*, August 1984)

▲ 2.4

Problems of urbanisation

Since the 1950s there has been a big increase of people moving from the country into the towns. This has caused overcrowding, disease, poverty and unemployment in many cities in the world.

Bombay

These are not new problems for some cities, however. They started in Bombay in the 1800s when thousands of workers came from the countryside to work in the cotton mills. The problems of overcrowding continue today. There are great contrasts between rich and poor. These can be seen in the different types of 'housing'.

1. **Sleeping on the streets** is a way of life for 100 000 people, 2% of Bombay's population. Some people *choose* to live on the streets, for three reasons:
(a) they are near their place of work, usually the city centre or industrial areas where casual workers are needed;
(b) in the hot season sleeping out is often less unpleasant than sleeping in the crowded shanties (see 2.5);

▶ 2.5 Two types of living in Bombay: shanty dwellings and apartments. The workers who are building the apartments live in the home-made shanties

▶ 2.6 Chawl district, Bombay

◀ 2.7 Marine Drive, Bombay

▼ 2.8 Bombay

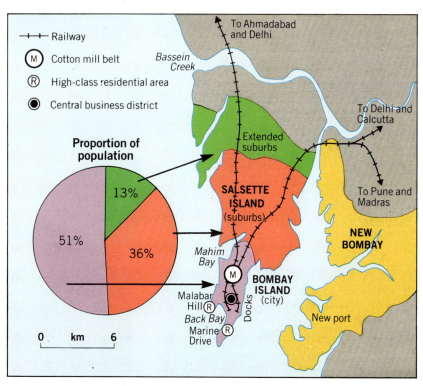

(c) in the wet monsoon period, many return to their villages to help with farming, taking with them money they have earned in the city.

2. **Shanty towns** (2.5) house 15%, or about 1 million, of Bombay's inhabitants. The largest of the shanty towns, on Mahim Bay (map 2.8), houses 300 000 squatters. These shanty towns lack sewage and other facilities and are liable to be blown down or flooded in the wet monsoon season. They are called *bustees* in Calcutta.

3. **Chawl districts** (2.6) house no less than 75% of Bombay's population. Built in the late 1800s, they were often of a good standard for their time. The ground floors have been converted into shops. Above there are one room tenements, each room sleeping up to ten people. Although there is indoor sanitation, each toilet may serve up to 100 people. The chawl districts are mostly on Bombay Island (map 2.8). As the pie chart beside the map shows, over half Bombay's people live in this very small area. In the mill district (M), densities of population reach 250 000/km^2.

4. The more **affluent** of Bombay's population, about 10%, live in blocks of flats in the Malabar Hill and Marine Drive (2.7) areas (map 2.8), or in the outer suburbs, from which they can commute by train.

The shanty towns of South America

The widespread movement of people from the drought and poverty of rural areas to all the cities of South America has led to major social, economic and cultural problems.

Social problems

In the cities of South America, the percentage of people suffering poor living conditions is smaller than in Indian cities. There is, however, still a tremendous gulf between the living conditions of the rich and those of the poor. The rich live in luxury apartments near the centre of cities or in affluent suburbs (2.9). The poor survive in appalling slums, often made by the people themselves, out of short-life materials such as cardboard, sacking, wood or corrugated iron. These houses make up the **shanty towns**, called *favellas* or *barriadas* in South America. There are, however, prospects for improvement.

When they first arrive, the migrants who pour into the city in a never-ending stream may find temporary accommodation with people they already know, who may have come from the same village. But they cannot stay long with friends, because they add to the overcrowding.

They then build makeshift shanty towns, which are uncontrolled developments by squatters on land they do not own. In 1970, over one-third of Lima's population lived in shanty towns or barriadas (2.10).

These barriadas are not necessarily permanent, however. The squatters have often to oppose attempts by the local authority to move them out. Once they feel secure, and have saved a little money from employment, they try to build more durable homes, from brick and concrete. These more permanent residential areas are known as *pueblos jovenes* (young towns). They can be seen in 2.11 (Lima) and in more detail in 2.12

▶ 2.9 Affluent suburbs, Lima

▼ 2.10 Barriada: new shanty town, Lima

▼ 2.11 A well-established poor suburb of Lima (Barranco)

▲ 2.12 Improved housing in Bogota, Colombia

(Bogota in Colombia). Notice how much better the construction of houses is in 2.12 than in 2.10. Notice also the regular road pattern in 2.11. At this stage, the local authority may supply electricity (see 2.11) and other services.

The change from barriada to pueblo joven is therefore a sign of progress. Despite the appalling overcrowding, poor sanitation and fire hazards, these are seen as 'slums of hope'. There is a chance that the family's prospects will gradually improve, if not for the parents, then for the children. One reason for this is that educational provision is better in the towns than in the country.

Economic problems

There is a high level of **unemployment**, because the local labour market often cannot cope with all the newcomers. New migrants often start off with casual employment: as garden workers, in catering, as labourers in the construction industry, in domestic work, or taking in laundry. If successful, they aim then to set up a small business, such as making furniture from packing cases, or running roadside stalls (2.13). Success depends both on hard work and luck. If it comes, the children might be provided with a better education and get apprenticeships or other qualifications. The number of unemployed is enormous, however, and it is likely that improved prospects will only be enjoyed by the minority.

▼ 2.13 Street traders in Lima

17

Cultural problems

It is said that when the rural migrants meet the 'bright lights' of the big city they become unsettled. They see expensive consumer goods in the shop windows of the city centre (2.14) which only the well-to-do can afford. This may add to the frustrations of living in the city. Contacts with friends and relatives in the countryside are often broken, and rural areas become poorer. The towns draw in young people from the countryside. It is difficult to get people to move from the towns to the countryside. As a result rural areas find themselves short of able-bodied workers, doctors and teachers.

2.15 is a map of Lima, showing how slum areas and the pueblos jovenes have been concentrated in areas away from those in which the wealthy live. These poor areas are often near unhealthy industrial zones, and on steep hill slopes, difficult to get to.

Advantages of urbanisation

1. As we have seen, shanty towns and pueblos jovenes are seen by their inhabitants as places in which there is at least some **prospect for family advancement**.

2. Urban development usually stimulates the economy of a developing country: for example, by providing **a market for agricultural produce**.

3. Although **urban employment** is often casual and poorly paid, it **brings in more income** than can often be obtained in rural areas.

4. While **shanty town services** are poor, they are often **better than those of the villages**. Note again the roads that the municipal authorities have built on 2.11 and 2.12. Educational and medical services are also more widely available.

▼ 2.14 Shopping street, central Lima

▼ 2.15 Land-use zones, Lima

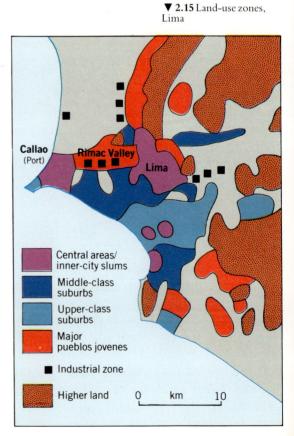

3 Rich and poor worlds

◀ 3.1 A family meal, Mali   ▲ 3.2 An English family tea

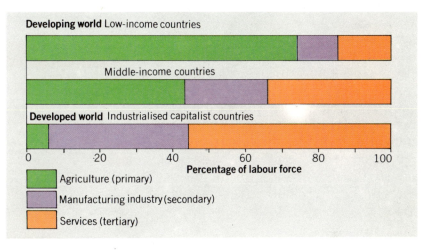

▲ 3.3 Structure of world production (1979)

Developed and developing countries

The two photographs (3.1 and 3.2) illustrate the enormous difference between the rich and poor countries of the world. 3.1 shows the main meal of the day for a family in Mali, one of the poorest countries in the world, in the Sahel area of Africa (4.12). It consists of millet, gruel and any scraps of meat or vegetable that are available. 3.2 shows the kind of meal many families can afford in Britain.

The developed world is made up of the rich industrialised countries, including North America, Western Europe, Australasia, and (somewhat less rich) the communist countries of Eastern Europe and the USSR. Among oriental countries, it includes Japan.

The developing world, sometimes known as the 'Third World', consists of two groups of countries:

(a) the very poor or **low-income countries**, such as Bangladesh and Mali;

(b) the fairly poor or **middle-income countries**, such as Peru, Bolivia and the Caribbean islands.

A **developing country** has the following characteristics, more strongly felt in the low-income countries.

1. Most of the people earn a living by **primary production**, mainly agriculture. 3.3 shows that nearly 75% of the labour force is engaged in such activity in the low-income countries, as against just over 40% in the middle-income countries, and only 6% in the developed world. The staple foods are provided by **subsistence farming**: that is, farming for the family's own consumption. This usually yields an inadequate and poorly balanced diet. 3.4 shows a landscape of subsistence farming in the Andes region of Bolivia. Notice the simply built farmhouses, and the small fields on the foothill slopes behind, with thin rocky soils.

19

2. Most of the people are **extremely poor** and cannot afford the facilities which people in the developed world regard as basic necessities: decent housing and sanitation; efficient medical services and educational provision.

3. Because of the lack of such facilities, **disease and illiteracy** are quite normal. **Infant mortality**, that is the death of children in infancy, is high.

4. Even so, high birth rates, as we saw in Chapter 1, maintain **rapid rates of population increase**. A large percentage of the population is less than fifteen years of age. The world's low-income countries have the biggest populations to support (see 3.5). Although there are large numbers of people in the developed world, there is a much greater income to support them.

3.6 is a map which shows the low-income and middle-income countries of the world. It divides the countries of the developed world into three types: (a) industrialised countries; (b) the oil-rich states of the Arab world; (c) communist countries.

▲ 3.4 Farming land, Bolivia

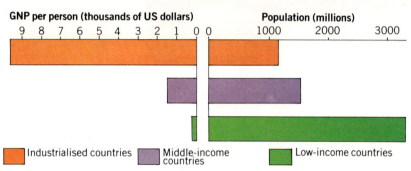

The GNP (gross national product) measures the wealth of a country. It is the yearly income.

▲ 3.5 Poverty and population (1980)

▼ 3.6 Developed and developing countries

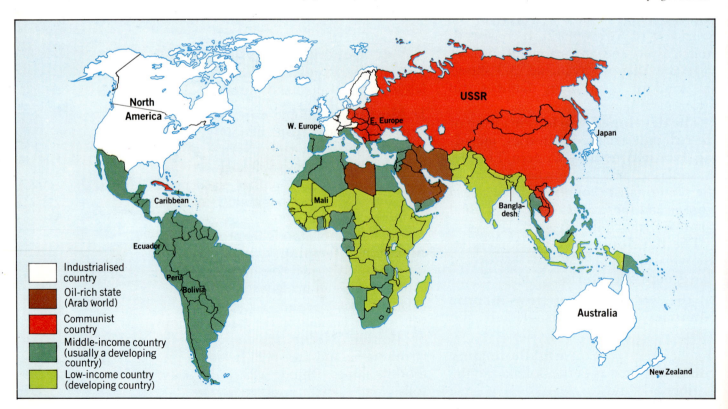

Measuring rich and poor

The most frequently used measure of a country's richness or poverty is the **gross national product** (GNP), which is the income of the country. It is the total value of goods and services produced by the country's economy over a period of one year. It is normally measured per head of population in US dollars ($). 3.7 compares the GNPs of developed and developing countries.

Low-income countries are those with a GNP of less than $1000 per head (per capita) of population. They are mostly in Africa and South and South-east Asia (3.7). They include all the Sahel countries of Africa; India, Pakistan and Bangladesh; and all South-east Asian countries apart from Malaysia and Singapore. Often political conflict has made worse the already bad conditions created by natural hazards such as drought.

Middle-income countries are those with GNPs of between $1000 and $6000 per capita (3.7). They are mainly in Latin America, North Africa, the Middle East, and a few states in the west and south of Africa. These countries contain large numbers of poor people, but usually have the advantage of additional resources, such as mineral wealth or plantation agriculture. Malaysia, Iraq and Venezuela are examples.

The **high-income countries** of the developed world are in four main groups:

(a) the **Western (Occidental) capitalist world**;

(b) certain **communist countries**, such as the USSR;

(c) some **oil-rich Arab states**, including Libya;

(d) **Japan**, and to a lesser extent, Hong Kong, in the **Eastern (Oriental) world**.

These countries usually have only a small percentage of the population working in primary production and large percentages in secondary and tertiary production (3.3). Manufacturing is very productive and highly mechanised, and creates great wealth. Similarly the highly developed tertiary activities foster trade and widen opportunities for employment, again creating wealth.

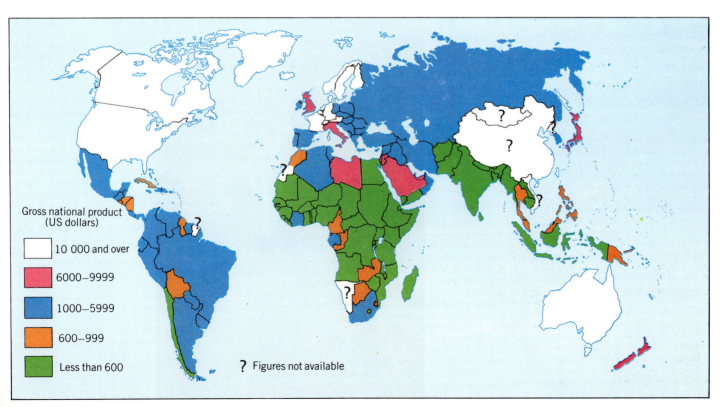

▼ 3.7 Gross national product per head of population

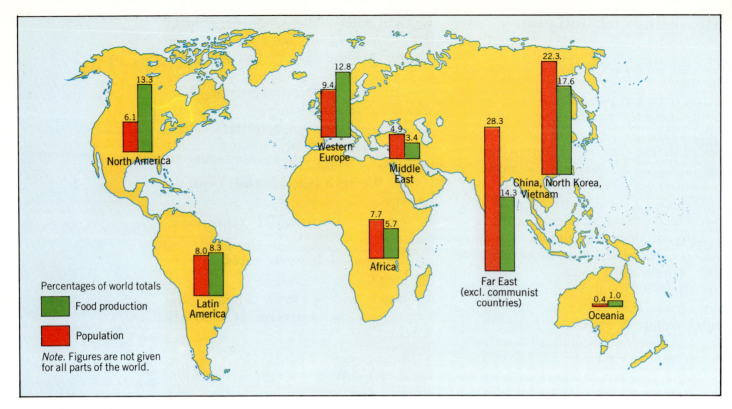

Food supply

Apart from overcrowding in towns and cities (see Chapter 2), one of the great problems facing developing countries is that they do not produce enough food for their growing populations. 3.8 makes it clear that North America and Western Europe produce a much greater proportion of the world's food supply than they have of the world's population. The reverse is the case in Asia and Africa, where many countries are low-income countries. In Latin America, the proportions are matched. As we have seen, most Latin American states, though developing countries, are middle-income countries, better supplied with food than the low-income countries.

Agriculture in these areas, as already noted, is **subsistence agriculture**. It is also **labour-intensive** agriculture, meaning that it relies on a large workforce of farmers. Look back at 1.5 and think of the vast amount of effort that went into preparing the terraced rice fields. Look also at the effort being put into ploughing the steep slopes of the Andean region of Ecuador on 3.9.

Another interesting feature of this photograph is the **low level of technology** shown, in this case the simple method of ploughing. Slopes such as these are often too steep for tractors and, in any case, many individual farmers would not be able to afford them.

▲ 3.8 World population and food supply

◄ 3.9 Traditional ploughing, Ecuador

Sometimes subsistence farmers do have produce to spare, which they sell in the markets of nearby towns. 3.10 again shows the simple nature of the transport used, in this case a bullock cart taking produce into an Indian city. 3.11 is a colourful street market with local produce in Jaipur in India. There looks as if there is quite a lot of food available, but it must be remembered that cities such as Jaipur have over half a million people to feed. Food supplies are not always reliable, especially where the monsoon rains fail.

Increasing food supplies

One way of meeting the problem of feeding the world's increasing population is to limit the number of births. Another is to increase food production. This can be achieved in various ways.

1. One is to **extend the area of agricultural land**. This can be done by (a) **drainage**, reclaiming land under water, as has happened in the developing world in the Netherlands; (b) **irrigation**, which allows barren dry areas to be cultivated, as in the Negev desert of Israel; and (c) **terracing** (see 1.5), which allows the use of steep slopes, especially for rice cultivation.

2. A second method is to **increase yields** of crops, so that the same areas can grow more. This can be achieved by the following.

(a) The use of **fertilisers**, which put plant nutrients into the soil, producing much better crops. But these are expensive and are much more used in the developed than in the developing world.

(b) **Crop spraying** with insecticides, which kill off the pests that destroy the crops. One efficient method is by spraying from the air. Again, it is the richer countries of the world that can afford such methods to improve their yields.

(c) Developing **higher-yielding varieties** of seeds. This has been termed the **Green Revolution**. It has resulted

◀ 3.10 Bullock and cart, India

◀ 3.11 Food market in Jaipur, India

in improved yields in countries such as Britain, and among richer farmers in the developing world. But it is expensive, partly because these higher-yielding seeds are dependent on the use of irrigation, pest control and fertilisers to be effective. The Green Revolution has therefore not helped poorer farmers much. More than three-quarters of the world's rice farmers have been unable to adopt the new varieties of seeds for these reasons.

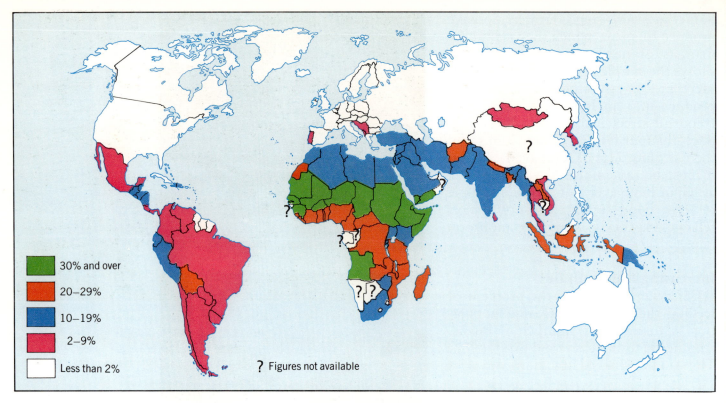

Health

Overcrowded living conditions and poor diet usually cause ill health. Poverty is associated with poor health and disease, and wealth with good health.

Life expectancy (the average age at which people die) has improved in all countries since 1900, as the following table shows.

Year	Developed world	Developing world
1900	50 years	23 years
1970	70 years	50 years
1979	73 years	59 years

There are still, however, some low-income countries (for example, in the Sahel) where life expectancy is less than fifty years. Improvements in medical care increase people's chances of living longer. But this can sometimes create other problems. Lower death rates, like higher birth rates, increase the population and mean more mouths to feed.

Infant mortality (the percentage of children who die before the age of four) remains high in many low-income countries. As map 3.12 shows, the worst areas are the Sahel countries and Angola in Africa, and the Yemen in the Arabian Peninsula. Here death rates for 1–4 year olds are over 30% and even over 40%. This means that on average, for every 100 children born, over 30 are likely to die before four years of age.

One reason for high infant mortality is **lack of doctors**. 3.13 is a graph showing the number of people per doctor in low-income, middle-income and developed countries. This ranges from one doctor for every 70 000 people in Ethiopia, to one doctor for every 350 people in the USSR. In the UK there is one doctor for every 750 people.

▲ 3.12 World infant (aged 1–4) mortality rate

◄ 3.13 Number of people per doctor

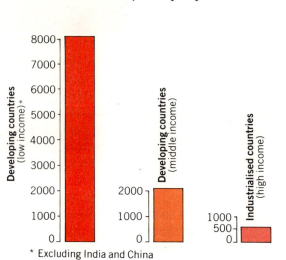

Diet

A satifactory diet is vital to good health. The poverty of developing countries causes poor diets, which do not contain enough of the following.

- **Calories:** 2450 calories per day are needed for good health; the average intake is about 2000 calories in the developing world, as against 3600 in the developed world.
- **Proteins:** the average intake is 50 grams per person in the developing world compared with 110 grams in the developed world.
- **Vitamins:** these are best provided by fresh fruit and vegetables, in short supply in the developing world.

As we have already seen (3.1, 3.2), the diets of the developing countries are *monotonous* compared with those of a developed country of the Western world. Monotonous diets are usually poorly balanced. As a result **dietary deficiency** diseases (**malnutrition**) occur, including (i) **kwashiorkor**, a protein deficiency disease; (ii) **marasmus**, a calorie deficiency disease. These diseases reduce resistance to infection, resulting in high infant mortality and, in the older age groups, a less efficient workforce.

Ways of improving diet

1. It is very important to **increase the quantity, quality and variety of food** produced but this is more easily done in the developed than in the developing world.

2. In the long term, successful **family planning** programmes will reduce demands on food supplies, and help to improve diets.

3. In the medium term, an important means of improvement is through health programmes which provide **supplementary feeding** of high-protein foodstuffs to children (3.14).

4. In the short term, food supplies may become so inadequate that **famines** result. We shall see in later chapters that this can be through natural or human hazards. People crowd into refugee camps and feeding centres to keep themselves alive. The only short-term solution here is to take advantage of **international aid**, from official organisations such as the United Nations, and from voluntary groups such as Oxfam (3.15).

▲ 3.14 Supplementary feeding, Maharashtra, India

◄ 3.15 Oxfam appeal

Infectious diseases

Apart from the diseases caused by poor diet, the people of developing countries continue to suffer from a whole series of infectious diseases which in many cases have been eliminated in the developed world. The following types occur.

- **Intestinal diseases**, such as dysentery and cholera, which are transmitted via inadequate sanitation and polluted water supplies, particularly where sewage enters water that is also used for drinking and bathing (3.16).
- **Airborne diseases**, such as influenza, smallpox and measles, which are spread by inhaling germs from infected persons.
- **Vector-borne diseases**, such as malaria, sleeping sickness and river blindness, which are carried by insects.

Some of these diseases are *endemic* (that is, normally present) in particular areas; for example, river blindness in the Niger River area of West Africa (3.17).

Economic costs of poor health

As 3.18 shows, there is a 'vicious cycle' of poverty in most developing countries. Poor health reduces the capacity for work, which in return reduces agricultural productivity, which in turn leads to poor diet. The circle is completed by the poor diet causing poor health. In addition, it is very expensive for a country to treat large numbers of sick and undernourished people. Many cannot afford to do so, therefore the people continue to be sick and undernourished.

◀ 3.16 Bathing and drinking water, Bangladesh

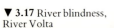
▼ 3.17 River blindness, River Volta

▼ 3.18 'Vicious cycle' of poverty

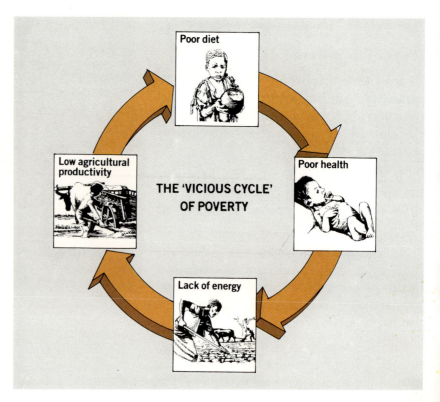

Ways of improving health

1. One of the most important means of promoting better world health is to **improve water supplies**. The need is to separate supplies used for drinking from those used for washing and sewage disposal. The walk to the river to collect drinking water can be replaced by the safer and more accessible *concrete-lined well* (3.19).

2. **Improved vaccines** help to combat infectious diseases. The developed world has shown that many diseases can be eradicated in this way. Unfortunately, in some cases strains of insects which are resistant to these vaccines have developed, which means that vaccines are no longer effective.

3. **Primary health care** is another important means of improving health, especially in rural areas, where there are not enough doctors to go round. Under this method, **health promoters** are trained to do such things as immunisation, attending childbirth, and taking blood samples (3.20). They are able to diagnose more serious cases which then can be sent to a town where there is a hospital and trained doctors. Many countries are also setting up **local health units** which are run by health promoters and provide the first-level primary health care service. Burkina Faso plans one such unit to serve a radius of 20 kilometres and 20 000 people. This is a very poor level of coverage, but better than previous provision.

◀ 3.19 Concrete-lined well, Burkina Faso

◀ 3.20 Health promoter, Sri Lanka

▼ 3.21 Percentage of population who are under 19

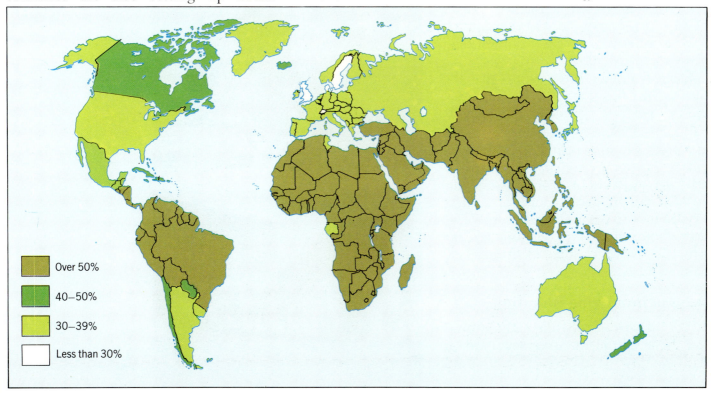

Education

As 3.21 indicates, in almost all of Africa, South and South-east Asia, and much of Latin America, over 50% of the population is less than 19 years old. This puts great strain on the educational systems of these poor countries.

Education is a luxury for many children in the developing world. Almost all children in most developed countries learn to read. But this is true of less than half of those in most low-income developing countries. Older children are even less likely to go to school than younger children. For example, in the countries of the Sahel and central Africa:

- nearly 50% boys and less than 35% of girls were enrolled at primary level;
- about 30% of boys and less than 20% of girls were enrolled at secondary level;
- about 5% of males and only about 2% of females were enrolled in higher education.

The expense of providing educational facilities is not the only reason for this. Many parents prefer to keep their children at home to help with family work. This is particularly true of girls in certain countries. In Moslem countries of Africa, for example, girls have much poorer educational opportunities than boys.

Lack of money often means that the quality of educational facilities is poor. 3.22 shows a very simple, brick-built, unplastered and unpainted urban school in a poor area of Calcutta. 3.23 shows a village school in the dry Baluchistan province of Pakistan, where lessons can be held out of doors. 3.24, of a rural school in Ethiopia, illustrates the fact that schools often have only one teacher who has to teach children of all ages.

Ways of improving education

1. As the cost of providing education is the main problem, **overseas aid** is needed.

2. As many developing countries have a widely scattered population, it is difficult to locate schools in rural areas that are within travelling distance of children. Possible solutions are to provide **boarding schools**, or **correspondence courses**. But these too are costly.

3. Many agree that it is vital to improve the **education of girls**, who, as we have seen, in many parts of the world are less well provided with education than boys. Where women are better educated, marriage take place later. This and increased knowledge of family planning reduces birth rates. But there are strong prejudices in many countries against the education of girls.

◀ 3.22 Urban school, Calcutta

◀ 3.23 Village school, Pakistan

◀ 3.24 All-age rural school, Ethiopia

4 Natural disasters

Natural disasters, such as earthquakes, volcanic eruptions, cyclones, floods, droughts and plagues of insects, occur all over the world, but the developing world has more than its fair share of them.

Earthquakes and volcanic eruptions happen, in particular, in areas surrounding the Pacific Ocean, for example in Latin America and South-east Asia. Two terrible examples occurred in 1985. The Mexico City earthquake was the worst Mexico had experienced this century. Many thousands were killed as the earthquake caused high-rise buildings to collapse in the city centre. An even worse disaster occurred in Colombia two months later, when the volcano Nevada del Ruiz erupted. It caused a vast mud slide which buried the town of Armero in the valley below, killing over 20 000 people. We shall look in more detail at the effects of two earlier disasters.

Cyclones and floods are a common feature of the monsoon lands of South and South-east Asia. We shall be looking at the effects of these in Bangladesh. Drought has been a serious problem in parts of Africa in recent years. Here too insect pests such as the locust ruin crops. We shall look at the effect of these problems on the Sahel countries of Africa.

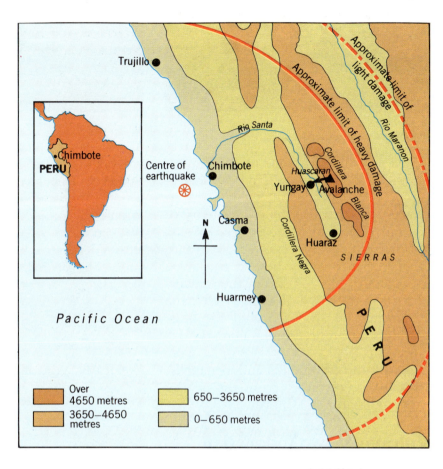

▲ 4.1 Chimbote earthquake, 1970

Earthquakes: Peru

At 3.23 p.m. local time on 31 May 1970, a major earthquake shook a large part of west central Peru. Its centre was in the floor of the Pacific Ocean, just off the port of Chimbote (4.1). Most of the buildings in nearby towns were made of mud blocks and were destroyed. 4.2 shows some of the severe damage caused in Chimbote. Serious structural damage was also caused in the coastal belt from Trujillo in the north to Huarmey in the south.

But worse was to happen in the mountains away from the coast. Here,

▲ 4.2 Collapsed buildings in Chimbote, Peru

29

▲ 4.3 Yungay, Peru: car after avalanche

◀ 4.4 Yungay: boulder brought down by avalanche

in the Cordillera Blanca of the Andes, lies the highest mountain in Peru, Huascaran, 6768 metres high. The earthquake caused a fearsome avalanche of ice and rock which, at a speed of 480 kilometres per hour, crashed down into the Rio Santa valley below, causing a great loss of life. 4.3 shows the remains of a car in the town of Yungay after the avalanche. 4.4 shows one of the huge boulders brought down. Yungay was buried in rock. 25 000 people were killed by the earthquake and avalanche; 15 000 of these were from the nearby town of Huaraz (4.1) alone.

Volcanoes: two Indonesian islands

Krakatoa and Bali are two Indonesian islands, one at the western and the other at the eastern end of Java (4.5). The large number of volcanoes shown on the map indicates that Java lies on one of the world's major belts of volcanic (and earthquake) activity.

Krakatoa was a small island in the Sunda Strait between Sumatra and Java. On 27 August 1883, it was the scene of one of the most violent volcanic eruptions in the world's history. Picture 4.6 shows Krakatoa before the great eruption. The eruption had the following effects.

1. The surface of the island was more or less blown away, leaving a large cavity under the sea, 300 metres deep.

2. Heavy volcanic material deposited

▼ 4.5 Krakatoa and Bali, off Java

▲ 4.6 Krakatoa before 1883

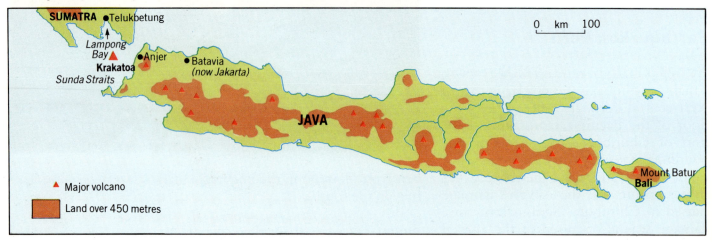

near the eruption increased the areas of nearby islands, and buried their forests.

3. A vast cloud of dust was carried far and wide in the air, blackening the sky, and causing lamps to be lit at mid-day in Batavia (Jakarta). The dust later gave rise to brilliant sunset and sunrise effects over many parts of the world.

4. The tremendous noise of the explosion was heard as far away as Australia and Ceylon (now Sri Lanka).

5. The most devastating effect, however, was on the waters of the ocean. A succession of huge tidal waves (or *tsunamis*) was generated, up to 35 metres high. These overwhelmed 300 towns and villages on the coasts of Java and Sumatra, killing 36 000 people.

6. The volcano erupted again in the 1920s, and a new island arose from the sea as a result, named Anak Krakatoa ('Child of Krakatoa').

Fortunately, not all volcanic eruptions are so devastating. Unlike earthquakes, volcanoes can have beneficial effects. 4.7 is a photograph of the volcano Batur on Bali. Notice the village in the foreground, and the cultivation terraces in the middle distance. Bali is a densely populated island. One of the reasons why so many people choose to live near an active volcano is that the lava that flows out of the volcano breaks down to form a fertile soil. This, combined with the heavy rainfall, supports rich agriculture, producing rice and plantation crops such as coconuts, sugar and coffee.

Cyclones and floods: Bangladesh

4.8 is a map of Bangladesh showing that most of the country is made up of the joint deltas of the rivers Ganges, Brahmaputra and Meghna, at the head of the Bay of Bengal. After the monsoon rains, these rivers *flood* in late summer and autumn. The floods are vital to the country's agriculture, as they lay down silts which renew soil fertility and allow as many as three crops of rice per year to be grown. The vegetation has adapted itself to the 'amphibious' environment of the delta lands (4.9). In some years, however (as in 1971 when over one-third of the country was under water), the floods can be devastating, causing serious damage and heavy loss of life.

4.10 shows the areas of the world affected by **tropical cyclones** or hurricanes. These create devastating storms in which winds can sometimes reach

▲ 4.7 Mount Batur, Bali

▼ 4.8 Bangladesh

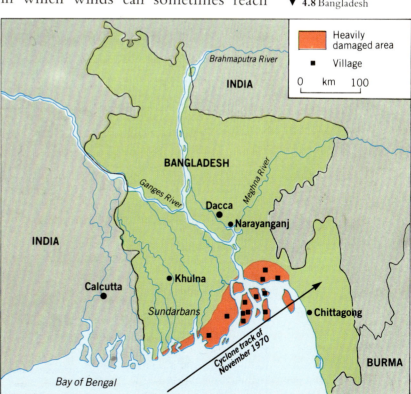

speeds of 300 km/hour. They are strongest over sea areas, but do tremendous damage to certain coastal areas. One of these areas is the Bay of Bengal, from which cyclones move towards the coast of Bangladesh (4.10), with its low-lying delta lands.

In November 1970, one of the worst natural disasters of the twentieth century struck. Violent winds hit the *Sundarbans* area (4.8), an environment of forests, swamps, rice fields and villages.

Roads, railways and bridges were destroyed and villages torn apart (4.11). The tidal wave (*tsunami*) which followed, up to 9 metres high, drowned vast numbers of people. In all, about 500 000 lost their lives, and 3.3 million were affected in the area shaded brown on 4.8. In May 1985 this same area was hit by another devastating cyclone. 17 000 homes were destroyed, 140 000 cattle lost, and up to 10 000 people killed.

◀ **4.9** The delta lands of Bangladesh

▼ **4.11** The aftermath of cyclone and flood, Bangladesh

▶ **4.10** Tropical cyclones

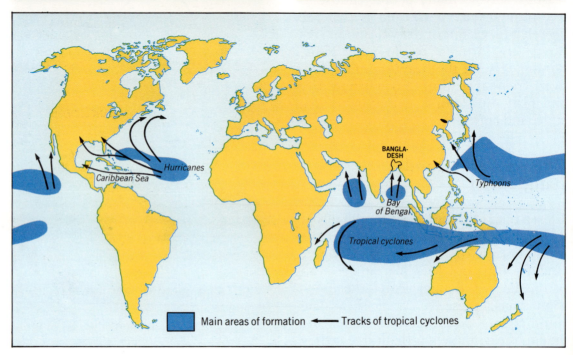

◀ 4.12 Drought hazard in the Sahel

▼ 4.13 Africa: vegetation zones

◀ 4.14 The Sahel after rain

◀ 4.15 Sahel drought: digging for water

Drought: The Sahel

The word 'Sahel' means 'border land' and, as maps 4.12 and 4.13 show, the Sahel countries are on the border between the Sahara Desert in the north and the savanna grasslands (with their higher rainfall) to the south. As we noted in Chapter 3, the people of these countries are among the poorest on earth. If they are lucky, onshore winds from the Atlantic Ocean (see 4.12) will arrive in the summer, bringing rain (4.14). Then their crops will grow and so will the grass which provides grazing for the animals. In bad years, dry winds blow from the Sahara Desert. Then the land becomes parched, the pools dry up, and people have to dig for water (4.15).

Rainfall totals in the Sahel have fallen steadily since the 1960s. For example, Mali (see 4.12) had 450 mm in 1958 but only 100 mm in 1984. (Crops are threatened when rainfall is less than 400 mm.) The Sahara Desert has 'marched south'. This has had a devastating effect on the nomadic (travelling) farmers of the region. Their animals have stripped the grass bare round the water holes (4.16), quickening the process of desertification. People have had to walk much further to find water, and may have had to leave their homes to look for food. In one year alone (1973), it was estimated that 100 000 people died from famine. The problem was worst for the nomadic farmers, whose animals died. Many were forced to live as refugees in camps on the edges of towns in countries such as Mali, Senegal, Chad and Burkina Faso. In 1973–4, the refugee camps of Mali contained 43 000 nomads who were dependent on food handouts. A further 28 000 camped in the food-growing areas. This made things more difficult for the settled farmers who were also affected by the drought, ran out of food and had to seek aid.

The high risk of drought remains. In Mali, for example, there were only two harvests between 1973 and 1984. Table 4.1 shows that overseas aid in the form of emergency relief goes only part way to meeting the problems of feeding Mali's population. Some countries, such as Ethiopia and Somalia are triply affected by poverty, drought, and by war and civil war. 4.17 is a picture of refugees from drought and war in Ethiopia.

▲ 4.16 Sahel: animals round a well

Table 4.1 Origin of grain consumed in Mali (thousand tonnes)

	1966	1973	1984
Home produced	1650	704	715
Imported	16	156	100
Aid	0	205	176

Population increase 1975–81 = 2.8% per year

Insect pests

As we have already seen (Chapter 3), insect pests are carriers of disease. One of the most serious of these diseases in the developing world is **malaria**. It is transmitted by the anopheles mosquito, which sucks the blood of an already infected person and then affects another person through its bite. Malaria is an energy-sapping illness, which seriously reduces people's capacity to work.

We are going to concentrate here, however, on two pests which affect crops and animals: the **locust** and the **tsetse fly**.

▲ 4.17 Refugees in Ethiopia

Locusts

4.18 shows the area in Africa affected by the desert locust. The Sahel countries are among those affected. Locusts were one of the plagues of Egypt, as recounted in the Book of Exodus in the Old Testament. They were seen as a punishment from God.

> 'And they shall cover the face of the earth, that one cannot be able to see the earth ... and shall eat every tree which groweth for you out of the field.'

34

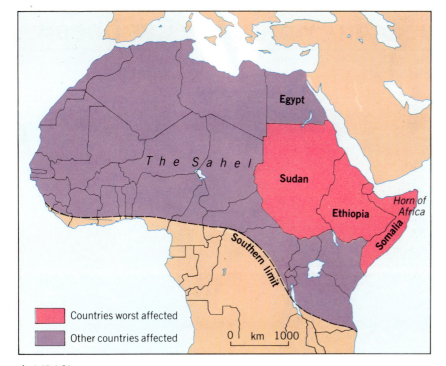

▲ 4.18 Africa: areas affected by the desert locust

As a result:

'there remained not any green thing in the trees, or in the herbs of the field, through all the land of Egypt'.

As 4.18 shows, Egypt is still affected today.

Locusts are a destructive breed of grasshopper which every so often migrate in swarms in unimaginable numbers, darkening the sky (4.19). Once started, a locust plague is almost impossible to stop, and any crops in its path are stripped bare. It is difficult to control the locusts in the breeding areas because huge expanses of land are affected.

Tsetse fly

The tsetse fly (4.20) is a blood-sucking insect, troublesome in the hotter parts of the day, which attacks both domestic animals and human beings. Tsetse flies abound where there is bush and forest, and on the edges of rivers, lakes and islands. They are found over large areas of West and Central Africa. They are not only annoying, but also dangerous in that they carry **trypanosomes**, which are responsible for fatal disease in domestic animals and humans. Strangely, although wild animals are 'carriers' of the disease, they are not effected by it. The loss of domestic animals has very serious effects on the economy of the herders of these regions.

The disease caused by trypanosomes is **sleeping sickness**. When it spread from West to Central Africa in the early years of this century, it caused great loss of life in areas in which the local people had no immunity. Between 1901 and 1906 it is thought that over 200 000 people died from sleeping sickness in Uganda alone. Again the vast area affected has made it very difficult to control the fly. The 'war on insects' has been going on throughout the history of humankind. Even modern technology in pest control has had only partial success.

▲ 4.19 Swarm of locusts

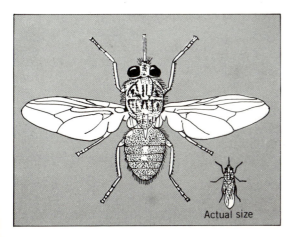

◀ 4.20 Tsetse fly

5 Tourism in the developing world: the Caribbean

The growth of international tourism

During the last thirty years or so there has been a vast increase in the international tourist industry. In 1950, there were 25 million international tourists. By 1975, the figure had inceased to over 200 million. More people are travelling abroad, and many are travelling long distances. The reasons for this growth in the tourist industry include:

- **rising living standards** in Western countries, with money to spare for expensive holidays;
- **the growth of air transport**, making fast long-distance travel possible;
- **the introduction of relatively inexpensive package holidays**, which cover fares, hotel costs and other expenses;
- **the development of facilities**, in particular high-quality hotels, to attract international tourists, backed by a lot of advertising.

Since the 1960s, tropical and sub-tropical countries in the developing world have tried to encourage tourism. These include countries of the Caribbean. The Caribbean is close to the southern USA so most of its tourists are American. However, many tourists come from Europe and Canada, despite the long distances that must be travelled. A popular method of holidaying in this sea and island world is to combine fast air travel to the area (often to Miami) with a more leisurely sea cruise round the islands (5.1).

5.1 shows the kind of route followed by the cruise liners. 5.2 is a picture of one of these liners at Nassau in the Bahamas. In the foreground is a beach

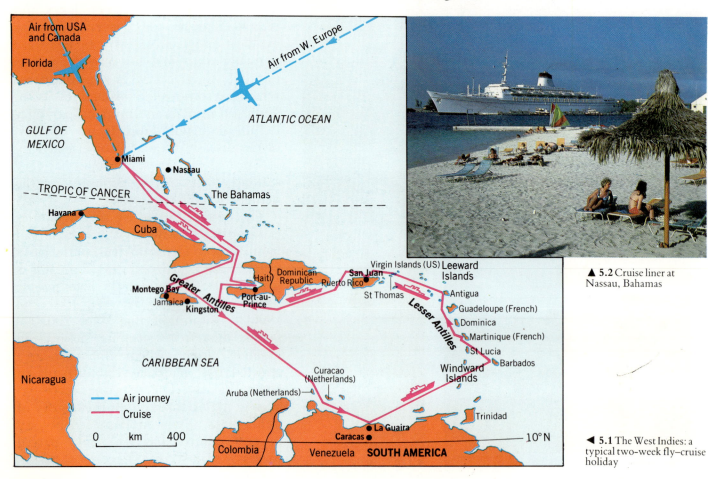

▲ 5.2 Cruise liner at Nassau, Bahamas

◀ 5.1 The West Indies: a typical two-week fly–cruise holiday belonging to one of the luxury hotels. Other liners by-pass the Bahamas and take the longer voyage into the islands of the Caribbean Sea. As the lines of latitude on the map indicate, these lie in the sub-tropical region, between the Tropic of Cancer and 10° north. The most important holiday islands are Jamaica; the US Virgin Islands; Antigua; St Lucia and Barbados (formerly British); and Guadeloupe and Martinique (French).

Barbados (5.3) provides a good example of the development of Caribbean tourism since the 1960s. In 1955, only 15 000 visitors came to Barbados. By 1965 the number had already risen to 68 000. In 1974, it was 230 000 and in 1980, 370 000.

What is it that attracts tourists to Barbados and other Caribbean islands?

1. The main attraction is perhaps the **tropical marine climate**. Sunshine and blue skies are usual (5.2). You can see on 5.4 that the average hours of sunshine are much greater than those of London. Temperatures are high, from 25 °C to 28 °C, but not excessive. Although hurricanes are a very occasional threat, the hot sunny weather is so reliable that it is a great attraction to tourists.

2. Equally important are the **natural features of the coasts**; clear blue waters, and clean sandy beaches backed by shady trees, as shown at Rockley Resort in Barbados (5.5). On this side of Barbados the waters are calm for sailing and swimming. 5.3 indicates that the main tourist areas are on the sheltered west and south-west side of the island, away from the prevailing north-easterly winds.

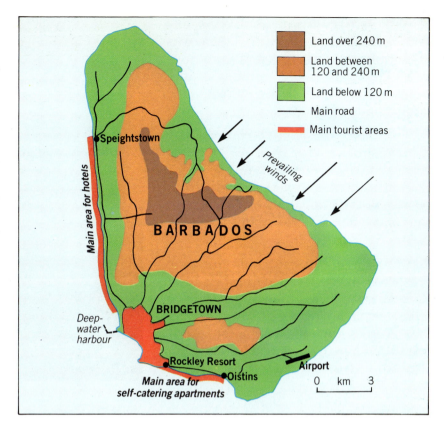

▲ 5.3 Barbados

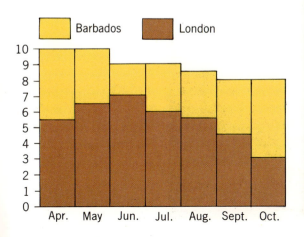

▼ 5.4 Average hours of sunshine, Barbados

▼ 5.5 Rockley beach, Barbados

3. Other attractive aspects of the **scenery** are tropical forests behind the coasts (5.6), volcanic peaks, such as Les Pitons in St Lucia (5.7), and unspoilt coastal fishing villages such as that shown in the foreground of 5.7.

4. The speed and relative cheapness of **air transport** is also vital. Air fares are kept as low as possible. In 1977, for example, an economy class flight from New York to Jamaica cost $334, and had only increased to about $350 by 1984.

5. The tourist industry could not have prospered, however, if **capital** had not been **invested** in building hotels and self-catering apartments. These attract the visitors, who come particularly from the United States and Canada, but also from Britain and other parts of

▲ **5.6** Coastal and volcanic scenery, St Lucia

◀ **5.7** Tropical vegetation, Jamaica

Western Europe and from the rest of the Caribbean (5.8). Barbados had provided about 9500 tourist beds by 1976. This had grown to 13 500 by 1981. Self-catering accommodation is increasingly popular. 5.3 shows that in Barbados the main hotels area is on the beautiful west coast, and the main area for self-catering apartments is near the capital Bridgetown (and Barbados airport). Many of the people staying in the hotels come off the cruise liners, which anchor in Bridgetown's deep-water harbour.

The facilities provided at Rockley Resort, apart from the beach (5.5), include:
- self-catering apartments, each with its own swimming pool, patio/balcony, private bath/shower, kitchenette, and air-conditioning;
- supermarket and gift shops;
- tennis and squash courts;
- saunas, restaurants and open-air bars;
- Rockley Beach Club (connected to the apartments by a free bus service), with an open air restaurant and other luxury facilities.

The tourist agencies also make sure that 'exotic' attractions are laid on for tourists, including local crafts and 'traditional' entertainments, such as steel bands (5.9).

Advantages of tourism to the islands

Before the coming of the tourist industry the economies of many Caribbean islands were insecure. They were over-dependent on plantation products such as sugar and bananas, or on mineral wealth such as bauxite in Jamaica. These products have always been at the mercy of fluctuating world prices.

The benefits of tourism include the following.

1. It helps to **balance out the economy**. The money that the tourists bring in is like an 'invisible export'. This is as valuable as money gained by real exports such as sugar. In 1974 Barbados earned almost as much from tourism as it did from its traditional plantation crop export, sugar. In 1979, tourism contributed twice as much as sugar to the gross national product (see Chapter 2) of the island.

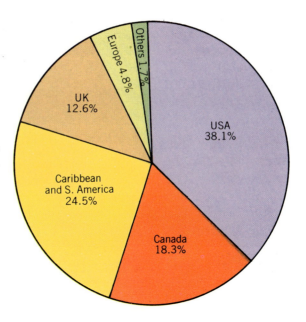

◀ 5.8 Origin of tourists visiting Barbados, 1984

▼ 5.9 Steel band, St Lucia

2. Tourism is also a **labour-intensive** industry. This means it provides many jobs and helps to **reduce** the serious **unemployment** on the islands. In 1974, tourism provided 12 000 jobs in Barbados in an overall workforce of 85 000. By 1979, the figure had increased to 15 000.

3. Tourism has also what economists call a **multiplier effect**. This means that it creates jobs not only directly (as, for example, waiters in hotels) but also indirectly, in servicing the hotels. For example, the hotels and apartments increase the demand for fish, agricultural products and crafts, thus providing extra work locally. Building of hotels and other facilities, such as roads and airports, gives a valuable boost to the construction industry.

Problems brought by tourism

The picture is not entirely rosy, however. Tourism has far from solved the economic problems of the Caribbean islands, as was thought possible in the early period of rapid growth. There are a number of reasons for this.

1. The **world recession** of the late 1970s and the 1980s has limited the growth of international tourism.

2. Tourism is a **seasonal occupation**, as graph 5.10 suggests. There are slack periods when less work is available, as in May–June and September–October in Barbados.

3. In some areas, the tourist industry concentrates on **lower-grade hotels** and apartments, and these provide **less employment** than the luxury end of the market.

4. The **cruise traffic**, calling in for a day or two at each port, **brings less money** to the islands than longer-stay holidays would do. Much of the eating is done on ship.

5. The luxury hotels tend to **buy a lot of produce** (in frozen form) **abroad**, which means local producers do not benefit.

6. Luxury hotels are expensive to build and need a **heavy capital investment**. This is difficult for small island governments to afford. Some say this investment would have been better placed in, for example, manufacturing industry.

7. Finally, it has also been argued that tourism **upsets the traditional culture** of the islands. It imports different sets of customs, and displays wealthy lifestyles (5.11) in the beach clubs and hotels, which are far beyond the reach of the local people. In addition, some hotels and clubs reserve areas of beach for their own visitors. The local inhabitants are excluded, and this leads to ill-feeling.

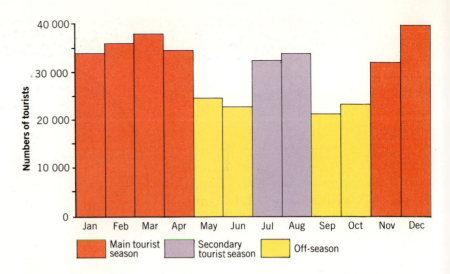

▲ **5.10** Number of tourists in Barbados, 1984

◀ **5.11** Wealthy tourist lifestyles, Barbados

6 Human conflict

Since human beings evolved on this earth, they have been in conflict with other human beings, either in groups or as individuals. One reason for this is the basic human need to survive, which involves finding food and shelter. People have been in conflict because they have been forced to *compete* for scarce resources. *Similar* people, grouped together in families, tribes or nations, aim to cooperate and share resources. Although there are sources of conflict *within* these groups (such as how the resources should best be shared), there are usually much greater chances of conflict *between* groups. **Diversity** (difference) is a major source of conflict.

We shall be looking at the following kinds of diversity in different parts of the world:

(a) religious difference;
(b) language difference;
(c) political difference;
(d) ethnic (racial) and cultural difference.

There is often an overlap between these types of difference. For example, different religious groups may (or may not) belong to different language and racial groups.

Religious difference

Human beings have always found their world mysterious and frightening, and often unsatisfying. Out of such feelings, and also a desire to explain what seems unexplainable, religions have developed. Tribal religions stretch back millions of years. But the great world religions came with the emergence of urban civilisations. 6.1, 6.2 and 6.3 are photographs of some buildings of worship associated with these world religions. 6.1 is a picture of the *Catholic* cathedral in Mexico City. 6.2 shows the Madurai Meenashki *Hindu* temple in India, while 6.3 is of two mosques in Cairo, belonging to the *Islamic* faith.

Among the Eastern religions, *Hinduism* is about 4000 years old and its offshoot, *Buddhism*, is over 2500 years old. The Chinese religions, of which *Confucianism* is the best known, are of similar age to Buddhism. These, like *Shintoism* in Japan, stress the worship of nature, ancestors and emperors, as against the worship of deities (Gods) in Hinduism.

◀ **6.1** Christianity: cathedral in Mexico City

▶ **6.2** Hinduism: temple in India

◀ **6.3** Islam: mosques in Cairo

The 'Western' religions emerged in the Middle East, and include *Judaism* (1300 B.C.), *Christianity* (early A.D.) and *Islam* (A.D. 630). These have spread over much wider areas. Christianity has been the most successful 'coloniser'. It has crossed many national and ethnic boundaries, as the Christian cathedral in Mexico City (6.1) shows.

Religious differences have often led to hatred and distrust between people. Throughout human history, millions of people have been persecuted and martyred for their religious beliefs. In recent times, the Jews were almost wiped out in Europe by the Nazis, for being a separate religious group which the Nazis thought was inferior. Israel is a state which was set up largely to receive the refugees from this holocaust. The Israeli people came from many different countries, but they are united by the religious belief of Judaism. Similarly, when Pakistan was separated from India in 1947, the basis of the division was religious: India largely Hindu, and Pakistan largely Moslem (Islam). Large numbers of people were killed in strife between these two groups at the time of transfer.

Language difference

Language is the basis of human communication and culture; the means of handing down ideas from generation to generation. Young children acquire the language of their culture from an early age and, through this, ideas and beliefs are transferred.

There are probably about 3500 languages in the world. Exploration and colonisation of other countries has resulted in a few of these becoming *world languages*, with English the most widespread. Nevertheless, language difference is a barrier to communication, and notices must often be printed in several languages.

6.4 shows a poster written in four languages, on display in Brighton, on the south coast of Britain. It warns

◀ **6.4** Multi-lingual poster, Britain

▲ **6.5** English and Chinese signs, Hong Kong

◀ **6.6** The languages of Apartheid, South Africa

people arriving from abroad that they cannot bring in domestic pets, because of the risk of rabies. 6.5 is a picture of a busy street in Hong Kong, with neon-lit signs advertising wares in both English and Chinese. Public signs in South Africa (6.6) may be in English, Afrikaans (a form of Dutch) and African languages.

Language differences have been, and continue to be sources of conflict. Belgium, for example, is divided on language grounds, into Walloon

(French)-speaking and Flemish (Dutch)-speaking areas, and there is much tension between the two. Similarly, in Canada there is trouble between French-speaking and English-speaking states. In Britain, pressure from the Welsh-speaking population has resulted in, for example, road signs in Wales being written in Welsh and English, and also a Welsh-speaking television channel.

Political difference

Over human history, peoples have grouped themselves together into separate states or nations. In the early days of urban civilisation, these were often city states. Some of these (for example, Ancient Rome) expanded, taking over other states, and built empires. Nation states have tended to group together in alliances, to help defend themselves against what they see as threats from outside states or groups of states.

An example of this today can be found in the conflict between the capitalist world and the communist world. Countries of Western Europe and North America have joined in the North Atlantic Treaty Organisation (NATO). Similarly the communist countries of Eastern Europe and the USSR have an alliance for mutual defence in the 'Warsaw Pact'.

The spread of communism

One of the most important political developments of the twentieth century has been the spread of communism (6.7). Communism is a set of political beliefs based on the socialist philosophy of a nineteenth-century German thinker, Karl Marx (Marxism). This states that there should be no private ownership of property and no social classes. All land, buildings, factories, etc. should be owned by the State, and wealth should be distributed equally among the people. Communism is opposed to the way in which capitalist societies are run.

6.7 shows how communist governments have spread over the world since the Russian Revolution of 1917 (6.8) when the luxurious Winter Palace of the Tsars (the monarchs) in Leningrad (6.9) was seized. After 1927, the Marxist government in the USSR 'nationalised' factories, mines, banks, trading companies, and the farming system. The farming system was 'collectivised'. The idea was to manage the whole means of production centrally, for the benefit of the state as a whole, and not for private

▼ 6.7 The spread of communism

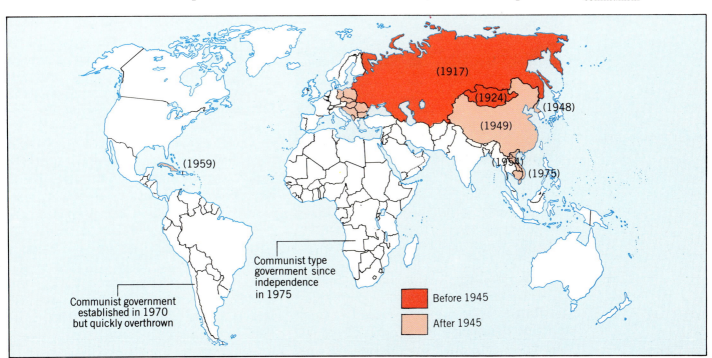

▶ 6.8 Fighting in the streets of Petrograd, 1917

◀ 6.9 Winter Palace, Leningrad

▶ 6.10 War memorial and post-war apartments, Leningrad

and there has been considerable progress in industry, particularly technology.

An important reason for the USSR's failure to achieve a higher rate of economic progress has been the amount of money it has spent on conflict with other countries. Defence against the German invasion during the Second World War cost the Soviets a great deal of money and many lives. Since then they have spend vast sums on defence, against what they see as the threat to their political system from the West. A striking feature of Russian cities are the many war memorials, commemorating the defence of the country against the German invaders. One is shown in 6.10, taken on the outskirts of Leningrad.

The chaos which followed the Second World War provided an opportunity for other communist revolutions. These occurred in Eastern Europe, China, North Korea and North Vietnam. As 6.7 shows, the communist countries form a compact group in Eastern Europe and Asia, including two of the largest countries in the world, the USSR and China. China has also the largest population, of about 1000 million. In the western hemisphere, Cuba is the only country with a well-established

profit. Many would argue that, from an economic point of view, the experiment has not been a success. For example, almost 70 years on from the 1917 Revolution, the USSR has to import large quantities of grain; and people's standard of living is generally much lower than in the West. There is, however, hardly any unemployment,

communist government. During the 1970s and 1980s, however, civil wars have taken place in several Latin American countries which are attempting to set up communist governments. In 1975, the communist North Vietnamese successfully took over South Vietnam after a war which lasted thirty years. In many conflicts in the developing world, particularly in Africa and Latin America, the USSR has provided support for guerrilla movements trying to overthrow dictatorships or Western-style democracies. The USA has provided support for existing governments and dictatorships, to stop the spread of communism.

In Europe, the main symbol of division between capitalist and communist worlds is the Berlin Wall (6.11). After the Second World War, Germany was divided into East Germany (communist) and West Germany (capitalist). The old capital of Berlin was also split into East and West, although it lies well inside the East German border. West Berlin is joined to the West only by a narrow corridor of communication links (road, rail, air) through East Germany.

The most serious threat to the future of humankind is that capitalist and communist worlds will come into open conflict, in a Third World War. Since the Second World War the USA and the USSR have engaged in a huge arms race. Each now has the capacity to destroy the human race in thermo-nuclear or biological warfare. At the end of the Second World War the first atomic bombs to be used against people were dropped on the cities of Hiroshima and Nagasaki in Japan. Of Hiroshima's 343 000 population, 66 000 were killed and 69 000 injured. Two-thirds of the city's buildings were destroyed. The atomic bomb devastated an area of about 10 km^2, an area equivalent to the centre of one of the world's great cities. A thermo-nuclear bomb (6.12) could destroy a whole conurbation, such as Greater London.

◀ 6.11 The Brandenburg Gate and the Berlin wall

Equally horrific are the after-effects of such weapons. As well as the people burned to death in the Hiroshima and Nagasaki fireballs, many died afterwards as a result of the radioactivity released by the explosion. The after-effects of a thermo-nuclear explosion would be far more widespread.

The debate about whether or not the arms race should be continued is of vital importance to humankind. Those in favour of it claim that these horrifying weapons are a *deterrent* to starting a war, because the effects of the weapons would be too dreadful to risk using them. Others argue that *disarmament* (getting rid of all nuclear weapons) is the only way to prevent their use. Mistakes can always be made, and there might be a government which is prepared to 'pull the trigger'. Also, if the nuclear arms race was stopped, the enormous amount of money saved could perhaps be used to help prevent *famine*: the other serious threat to the future of the world.

◀ 6.12 A thermo-nuclear test explosion, 1954

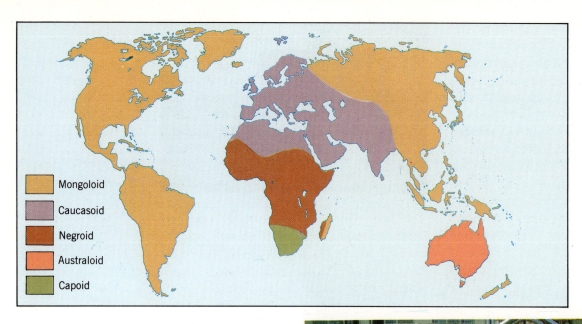

◀ 6.13 The major indigenous races of the world

▼ 6.14 Children of different races in a Nairobi suburb, Kenya

◀ 6.15 Children in a Calcutta park

◀ 6.16 Children boarding a school bus in Thailand

Ethnic (racial) difference

People are of the same race if they are descended from a common ancestor. The earliest people originated in East Africa, and spread out from there to all parts of the world. In adapting to different environments, human beings acquired different physical and cultural characteristics. This made the world a multi-racial place at an early stage of human development.

6.13 shows the world's indigenous races: that is, the original races found in particular parts of the world. Three major races have been distinguished.

(a) The **Caucasoid** race originally lived in Europe, North Africa, and South-west and South Asia. Today this race covers a variety of characteristics. For example, the white children on 6.14 and the Indian children on 6.15 are all derived from the Caucasoid race.

(b) The **Mongoloid** race originally lived in East and South-East Asia, and America. 6.16 shows Thai children of the Mongoloid race boarding a school bus. The original inhabitants of America include the Inuit (Eskimos), the North American Indians, and the larger

▲ 6.17 Amerindian farmer, Bolivian plateau

The children we see on 6.14, 6.15 and 6.16 will, *within* each racial group, have different heights and weights, and different levels of intelligence. The main difference *between* the groups is that children brought up in developed countries will usually have much better opportunities than those in the developing world. 6.14 is unusual, in that it shows black and white children playing together in a well-to-do suburb of Nairobi in Kenya. In the developing world a minority of children are privileged. In the developed world, there are a minority of children (often, for example, of immigrant families) growing up in the city slums, who are under-privileged.

One of the saddest facts of human history is that some groups have come to see themselves as racially 'purer' and superior to others, and have treated them cruelly. Most recently, this hap-

group of Amerindians who still inhabit Latin America (6.17 and 6.20). These have often mixed with other racial groups. The present inhabitants of North America include many Caucasoids and Negroids, as a result of mass migrations (see pages 10–11).

(c) The **Negroid** race originally lived in Africa south of the Sahara. Children of this group are shown on 6.14.

Two further sub-groups have been distinguished which today are small in number and have been driven into remote desert regions:

(d) the **Capoid**: Bushmen and Hottentots of South-west Africa:

(e) the **Australoid**: the Aborigines of Australia. (Most Australians today are of Caucasoid race, again because of migration from Europe.)

As the photographs show, these racial groups differ in physical appearance. There are variations in height, skin colour, head shape, and facial characteristics (eyes, nose and hair). But there are also major differences *within* these groups. As we have noted, the Caucasoid group includes Indians, Arabs and Europeans. Within Europe, there are recognisable differences between the darker-skinned and generally darker-haired Mediterranean peoples and the lighter-skinned and generally lighter-haired Scandinavian people.

▼ 6.18 Black slaves being landed at Jamestown, USA, in the early seventeenth century

pened in the Nazi persecutions of the Jews. It also happened in the colonisation of Africa, when Europeans, for their own profit, transported black people against their will to the Americas to be sold as slaves (6.18). We are going to look now at two other examples of racial or cultural oppression.

The Amerindians of Amazonia

The racial composition of South American countries such as Brazil is complex. As we have seen, the original inhabitants were the Amerindians of the Mongoloid race. These people developed advanced urban civilisations, before the coming of Europeans: for example, the Aztec civilisation of Mexico, and the Inca civilisation of the Andes, of which Cuzco, Peru (6.19), was the capital city. Many of its present-day buildings are built on Inca foundations. Pure-bred Indians are now mainly confined to more remote areas such as the Andes (6.17) and the Amazonian forests. Since the arrival and influence of Europeans, however, many such Indians have turned to 'European' ways of life and dress (6.20).

Amerindians have been brutally treated by incoming groups. The Spanish conquerors destroyed the great Aztec and Inca civilisations and took control of much of Latin America. The Portuguese occupied Brazil, and brought over negro slaves. There is now a mixed racial pattern in countries such as Brazil, which includes:

- people of European origin;
- people of Indian origin;
- mixed white-Indian people, or *mestizos*;
- people of African origin;
- mixed white-black people, or *mulattos*.

The Amazonian Indians are the only pure-bred Indians remaining in Brazil. They have been expelled from their homes and sometimes murdered by rubber collectors, ranchers and mining gangs.

▲ 6.19 Cuzco, Peru, former Inca capital

Many have been killed by 'Western' diseases such as smallpox and measles, to which they have had no immunity. Many have deserted their traditional ways of life, and can now be found living in squalor by the new roads which cross Amazonia. They have given up their traditional skills and, instead, the women and children beg by the roadside. Others have drifted to towns seeking casual work. Indian peoples in their 'natural' state, therefore, have largely disappeared from the Amazon Basin, apart from those surviving in remote forest areas. Most remaining now live on 'Indian reserves' set up by the Brazilian government.

▼ 6.20 Amerindians, Guyana

Apartheid in South Africa

Before European settlers came to South Africa, the early Bushmen and Hottentot (Capoid) peoples had been driven to remote areas of the Kalahari desert by incoming and more advanced Bantu (Negroid) groups. White settlers (Dutch and English) have in turn driven Bantu peoples into poorer parts of South Africa. The whites also brought in Asiatic people, largely to work on the sugar plantations. As a result, the racial composition of South Africa is complicated. It is:

- 71% black people;
- 17% white people;
- 9% 'coloured' people (of mixed race);
- 3% Asian people.

Language is a further complication. The Dutch settlers have maintained their identity, and Afrikaans, their language, is an official language (6.6). In addition, there are the Bantu languages and English.

Although the majority of the population is black, the political power is in the hands of the white minority. Fear of the blacks taking power has led the white rulers to adopt a *racist* policy (based on the view that one race is superior to another). This policy has two main aspects:

(a) *the use of migrant black workers* to provide the South African economy with a cheap unskilled labour force;
(b) *apartheid* (separate development) of whites and non-whites, both socially and geographically.

Migrant labour

Large numbers of black workers from nearby countries such as Malawi, Mozambique, Lesotho, Botswana, Zambia and Swaziland move to South Africa to work for many months of the year. A large proportion of these migrant workers are men who are forced by poverty to leave their families to find employment that is not available in their home country. They then send money back home to help their families.

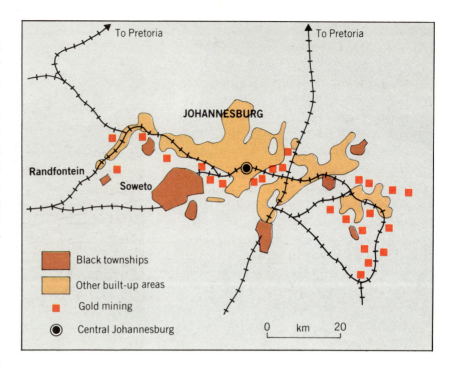

▲ 6.21 Witwatersrand conurbation

Most of them make for the Witwatersrand conurbation, centre of the wealthy gold mining industry (6.21). Since the late nineteenth century, black labour has been used in the mines which now supply about 70% of the non-communist world's gold.

The South African mining industry is still dependent on black labour, with nine blacks for every one white. The average income for a white worker is roughly fourteen times that of a black worker. Most of the migrant workers are men who are housed in hostels, where they sleep, cook and live in barrack-type rooms (6.22). A smaller

▼ 6.22 Mine workers' hostel

percentage of migrant workers are women, moving from their homelands to work as domestic servants or children's nurses with white families. They are separated from their husbands and their own children, if married. Such women are allowed to visit their families once or twice a year.

The use of migrant labour has the economic benefit of providing the family at home with more income than it would otherwise have (though still a poor income by European standards). But it results in an inhuman disruption of family life, and the white employers exploit the black workers by paying them very low wages. This enables South African goods to be sold cheaply abroad.

Apartheid (separate development)
This is a form of partition of the country, in which the black population is only allowed to live in special areas. These include what are in fact two types of slums.

1. **Rural slums**, or **homelands**, such as the Transkei, set up in 1976, Bophutatswana (1978), Venda (1980) and Ciskei (1981). These are agriculturally poor areas of the Veld (6.23), inadequate to feed their black populations at a decent level. They have high infant mortality rates and levels of malnutrition. Black families who used to live in 'white' areas are 'resettled' in villages or camps. They then have to fend for themselves, building homes from any material they can find.

2. **Urban slums**, or **townships**, can be found particularly in the Witwatersrand conurbation. Soweto is the largest black township, with over 1 million people (6.21). It is a wholly segregated black settlement, in which the best of the housing is made up of drab rows of box-like dwellings (6.24). Schooling and medical facilities are hopelessly inadequate. The people 'commute' to work in the Witwatersrand cities (6.25).

There is segregation in all aspects of daily living. Non-whites must travel on

◀ 6.23 Poor farming in a 'homelands' area

▼ 6.24 Soweto: black township

◀ 6.25 Black commuters arriving in Johannesburg

separate trains, and use separate restaurants, schools, sports facilities, etc. Black people are widely discriminated against. All blacks have to carry identity booklets stamped with permission to work in a particular place.

7 Environmental concern

Conflict between people and their **environments** is a world-wide problem. Human beings have become increasingly conscious of the need to protect the environment and **conserve its resources**. Some of these, such as oil, are being used up at an alarming rate. In developing countries the impact of human beings as destroyers or polluters of the environment can be particularly serious, because these countries do not have enough money to fight the problems very effectively. Here we concentrate on aspects of conflict and conservation that affect developing countries in particular, though they occur all over the world. We shall not deal with pollution and conservation in the industrialised world, nor with the destruction and conservation of life in the oceans.

Agricultural land

In the past century in particular, large areas of agricultural land have been destroyed by unwise methods of farming which lead to **soil erosion**. Soil erosion can be caused by the following.

(a) **Ploughing down the slope of the ground**. Where soil is exposed on a slope, heavy downpours of rain can lead to **gullying**. Water trenches form which grow and allow small river valleys to develop. When it rains, the soil is washed away downslope. Notice how the gullying on 7.1 is destroying scarce agricultural land in Lesotho in South Africa.

(b) **Planting crops in areas too dry** for arable farming.

(c) **Wind**. If the topsoil is exposed (perhaps through **over-grazing** of animals) and becomes dry, it can be blown away by the wind. **Wind erosion** has happened on a disastrous scale in the Sahel, through the combined effects of drought and over-grazing (4.16).

◀ 7.1 Gullying in Lesotho, South Africa

(d) **Clearance of trees**, for example for fuel (7.2). Absence of woodland increases the menace of wind erosion.

There are various ways of conserving soils:

- **contour ploughing**, which means that the furrows run across rather than down the slope;
- **terracing** (see 1.5), forming flat shelves on slopes, which prevent soil from being washed down;
- **afforestation**, providing windbreaks of trees or shrubs to limit the effects of wind erosion.

◀ 7.2 Collecting wood in Burkina Faso

Water supplies

The journal headline (7.3) draws attention to the polluted state of India's 'holy river', the Ganges. We have already noted in Chapter 3 the threat which **polluted water** poses to the health of people in developing countries (3.16). In India, hundreds of millions of Hindus believe that the water of the Ganges helps to wash away sins, and vast numbers of pilgrims come to the city of Varanasi (Benares) on the Ganges. Here conservationists have found that pollution is at its worst, and that the bathers (7.4) can develop nasty skin complaints. The pollution is a result of:

- contamination from riverside cremation grounds, where many bury the ashes of their dead;
- putting dead bodies in the water;
- untreated sewage from the cities of the Ganges;
- industrial waste (*effluent*) from factories.

Only eight of India's 142 cities were said to have effective sewage systems in 1980. 72 had no facilities at all.

Water pollution is widespread throughout the developing world. In rural areas, rivers and ponds are used for drinking, washing and sewage disposal. Shanty towns of urban areas often have no proper drinking water or facilities for washing and sewage disposal.

There are various ways to prevent pollution.

(a) Building *sewage systems* in urban areas, and demanding that industrial firms treat their effluent to make it safe. But this is an expensive process, so few firms do it.

(b) Building *concrete-lined wells* (3.19) to ensure pure water.

(c) Building *separate latrines* or other toilet facilities.

7.5 shows an interesting conservation scheme for a Sahelian village, designed to improve food, water and energy supplies, and prevent soil erosion and water pollution.

Pollution spreads to India's sacred river

The holy Ganges has recently been found 'unfit for bathing' by conservationists, and other rivers are in an even worse state.

▲ 7.3 *Earthwatch*, no. 30, 1980

▼ 7.4 Bathing in the Ganges at Varanasi

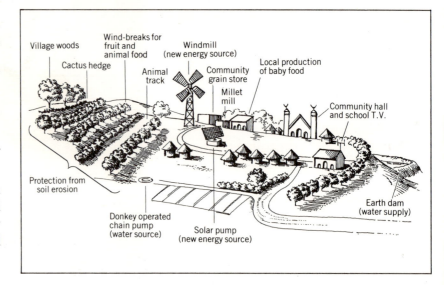

▼ 7.5 Conservation plan for a Sahelian village

◀ 7.6 The threat to the world's forest

Forests

7.6 is a cartoon depicting the cities of the developed world, with their huge demands for timber, newsprint, chemical raw materials, and various forms of paper, swallowing up the forest resources, many of which lie in the developing world. The **coniferous softwood forests** are mostly in the developed world (Canada and the USSR). Conservation of these trees is not a great problem because coniferous trees grow quite quickly (20 years). There are now extensive programmes of replanting, to maintain supplies of wood. This is not so easy with the **tropical hardwood forests** of the developing world, however, because these trees take far longer (100 years) to reach maturity. These forests are steadily being reduced in size as trees are cut down and not replaced.

The Amazon deforestation

One alarming example of **deforestation** is in the equatorial forests of Amazonia, the *selvas*. In Brazil a vast new highway system cuts across what was once an immense forest wilderness, accessible only by river. 7.7 shows how the north-west of the country is now crossed by roads. These are mostly not paved. They have a double layer of gravel topping or packed earth (7.8).

▼ 7.7 The opening up of Amazonia

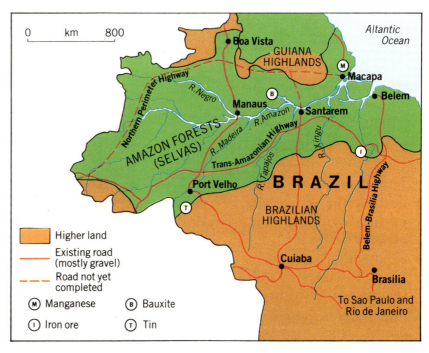

▲ 7.8 Amazonian highway near Manaus, Brazil

▶ 7.9 Forest firing, Amazonia

Building roads through thick forest is not easy. First the trees have to be cleared. Forest burning is the usual method. It is a common sight in Amazonia today (7.9 and 7.11), where trees are being cleared for the roads and for farmland. Once the trees have gone, heavy tropical rains turn the clay soil into a quagmire (7.10), which in this picture is blocking the progress of a local bus. Lorries carrying materials or workers required in the construction sites for new towns and mining camps are also delayed.

The Amazon area is being exploited for:

(a) timber and other forest products;
(b) valuable minerals, including tin, iron, manganese and bauxite (7.7 and 7.11);
(c) farmland for poor agriculturalists from drought-hit areas of north-east Brazil (7.12);
(d) land for wealthy cattle ranchers and plantation owners.

This deforestation will, it is argued,

- **destroy the world's largest source of hardwood timber**, almost impossible to replace;
- expose the clay soils to the heavy rainfall, which has already **caused serious soil erosion**;
- lead to more rapid run-off of rain, erratic river flow and **flooding**, which has already affected towns such as Manaus (7.7);
- reduce yearly rainfall and increase temperatures, which will gradually produce a **more arid environment**.

▼ 7.10 Bus stuck in mud, Amazonia

▲ 7.11 Clearing for new bauxite mining settlement, Brazil

▼ 7.12 Poor farmers on cleared forest land near Santarem, Amazonia

▲ 7.13 Reafforestation in Burkina Faso

Deforestation in South-east and South Asia

In more densely populated parts of the developing world, such as India and Indonesia, the threat to the forests often comes from the local people, who rely on the forests for **firewood** and in some cases **building material**. In response to a question on the main result of population pressure, an Indonesian Minister of State for the Environment replied:

"The pressure on the forest is tremendous. There is hardly any real forest left in the whole of Java. It covers less than 5 per cent of the land area, which is not good. We have tried planting fast-growing trees along the edge of the terraced land to control the run-off of water and so soil erosion."

Reafforestation

In the earlier section on soil erosion we noted the importance of planting trees (afforestation) to preserve the soil. **Reafforestation** (7.13) is the only safe way of keeping up the supply of timber. It is also vital to local people, who need the wood for fuel (7.2). 7.14 is a graph showing the numbers of people in developing countries with firewood shortages in 1980. The problem is that the replanted forest is not of the same quality as the original. The cleared areas at first resemble a bare lunar landscape. This is quickly overgrown. But it is overgrown by poorer **secondary forest**, which has fewer species of tree and will not produce such high-quality wood.

The rate at which the developing world is clearing the tropical forest is alarming. Athough vast areas of forest remain, the warning signs are clear. The forest environment must be conserved. Otherwise, not only will the world's wood supply fail, but soil erosion, flooding, drought, and even more general climatic change over the world, might follow.

▼ 7.14 Numbers of people facing firewood shortages, 1980

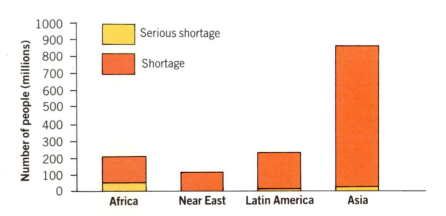

Wildlife

The relationship between wildlife and its surroundings is very finely balanced. On the savanna grasslands of Africa, for example, there is an enormous variety of wildlife, and the feeding habits of the different animals are often complementary rather than competitive. Among the **herbivores** (vegetation-eating animals), such as gazelles (7.15), different species live on a different range of food. For example:

(a) monkeys, giraffes and elephants can consume the higher-level branches of trees;

(b) zebra, buffalo and antelope share the lower branches and shrubs;

(c) smaller animals browse the bushes and graze on the grassland.

The herbivores are preyed on by the **carnivores** (meat-eating animals) such as lions, leopards, jackals and hyenas. When a large herbivore such as a zebra is killed, say by a lion, the lion will take the 'first choice' of meat. When it has enough for itself and family, packs of hyenas will move in, in some cases contesting the carcass with the lion. When these in turn have finished, vultures fly down, with beaks specially adapted to pick clean the carcass. When the birds have gone, carrion flies and beetles complete the process. Even the skeletons are attacked by horn-boring larvae.

Sometimes natural disasters disturb this balance, leaving too many animals for the land (perhaps ravaged by drought) to support. Many die through famine. Little can be done to prevent such disasters. More worrying is the killing of wildlife by people. This is often to satisfy the fads of Westernised consumer society. In Africa and Asia, for example, poachers have killed off large numbers of elephants for the ivory of their tusks; and leopards and crocodiles for their skins. The destruction of forest destroys the natural environment of wildlife. In this way, the Javan tiger has almost been wiped out.

▲ 7.15 Savanna wildlife: gazelles in a wildlife park, Kenya

Wildlife is an important resource for some countries, because it attracts tourists to the great nature reserves and parks, as in the savanna region of Kenya (7.15). Notice the local style of building for the 'safari hotel' (7.16).

Among the most important conservation measures are:

- **establishing national parks and reserves**, which are protected areas, now found all over the grasslands of Africa (7.15);
- **trying to stop rare species from dying out, by breeding them in captivity**, a task which is now being undertaken by many of the world's great zoos.

▼ 7.16 African game reserve

8 Interdependence

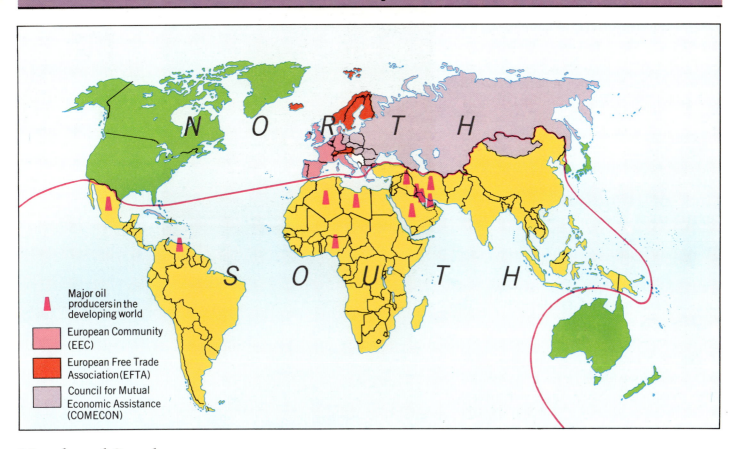

▲ 8.1 North and South: world trading blocs

North and South

In 1980, the Brandt Report, entitled *North–South: a Programme for Survival*, was published. It was the result of a special study on world interdependence, particularly in connection with trade, debt and aid. The Report divided the world into two halves, as shown on 8.1. 'The North' included all the countries of the industrialised developed world: all in the northern hemisphere except for Australia and New Zealand. Many countries of the North have grouped together for trading purposes. 'The South' included both the low-income and the middle-income countries (see Chapter 3) of the developing world.

Table 8.1 makes clear the great contrasts in economic prosperity and social well-being between the two, the South being deprived in almost every respect. According to the Brandt Report, about 800 million people, 40% of the South's population, are barely surviving. Most of these people live in the countries of sub-Saharan Africa (particularly the Sahel), and in South Asia, including India, Pakistan, Bangladesh and Indonesia. In some of these worst-affected countries, the problems have been increased by civil war, as happened in Bangladesh, Somalia, and Chad.

The idea of the Report came from an international organisation, the World Bank, in 1977. The group of people chosen to carry out the study was led by Willy Brandt, a former Chancellor of West Germany. Members included experts from many countries, both

Table 8.1

	North	South
Percentage of world's population	25%	75%
Percentage of world's income	80%	20%
Expectation of life	70 years	50 years
Percentage suffering from hunger	Almost nil	20%
Percentage who are formally educated	Virtually 100%	About 50%
Percentage of world manufacturing industry	Over 90%	Less than 10%
Percentage of world's multinational corporations	Virtually 100%	Almost nil

'North' and 'South'. The most important conclusion the Report came to was that the survival of humankind will depend on improved cooperation between the rich world of the North and the poor world of the South.

'Economic growth in one country depends increasingly on the performance of others. The South cannot grow adequately without the North. The North cannot prosper unless there is greater progress in the South.'

Lack of cooperation: unequal terms of trade

Cooperation between the countries of the North and the South has been, and still is, limited. One of the most important links is that of **trade**. There are various ways in which the countries of the South are at a disadvantage in this trade.

1. Many basic fuels, minerals, plantation productions and timber products come from countries of the South. These include oil, copper, tin, coffee, tea, bananas, rubber, jute, ground nuts (8.2) and tropical hardwoods. Many of these countries rely on the export of one or two of these items for earning foreign currency. For example, copper makes up 90% of Zambia's exports, and sugar 90% of those of Mauritius. It is very **risky for a country to rely on one product**. This is especially true of agricultural products, where a bad harvest can mean that vital export earnings are lost.

2. Countries that rely on one export product are also at the mercy of **fluctuating world prices**. Sugar, for example, varied in price from $1000 per tonne in 1974 to $200 in 1976, according to whether it was scarce or plentiful. In years of glut, it might not be saleable. Where this happens in developed countries, such as the USA, the product can be stored (8.3) until it is needed. But developing countries cannot afford to do this.

3. **Selling raw materials earns less**

◀ 8.2 Ground nuts awaiting export, Kano, Nigeria

◀ 8.3 Wheat storage, Oregon, USA

money than selling partly processed or fully manufactured goods. It is better, for example, to export jute cloth than raw jute. The South has less than 10% of the world's manufacturing industry. But when manufacturing industry *is* set up in developing countries, the North protests. The reason is that the South can sell manufactured goods more cheaply than the North because labour costs are cheaper. This competition means that the North would lose trade.

4. Because of this, **tariff barriers** are set up. For example, when crude palm-oil enters EEC countries from West Africa, it faces a 4% tariff (tax). If it is refined, there is a 12% tariff. This raises the selling price within the EEC but the West African exporters do not benefit from it.

5. The **rise in world oil prices** has had a damaging effect on developing countries which need oil and do not produce it themselves. In the early 1950s, for example, India's import bill for petroleum was less than 10% of the total. By 1975 it had risen to a crippling 26%. This meant India had to reduce imports of other vital products.

6. Finally, world trade is controlled in many cases by **multinational corporations**, which are all owned in the North. One London-based group, for example, comprises over 800 companies in over 80 different countries, both in the developed and developing world. The profits go mostly to the developed world.

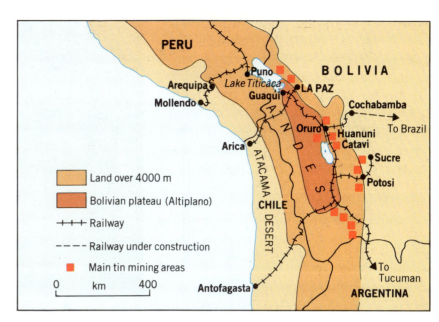
▲ 8.4 Tin mining in Bolivia

A case study: Bolivian tin

The tin mines of Bolivia are the highest in the world, found in mountains over 4000 metres high, overlooking the Bolivian plateau (8.4 and 8.5). Tin is the country's most important export but, although the tin ore is plentiful, production costs are high. This is because:

- the mines are often found in **remote mountain locations**, which increases the costs of transport;
- the **tin ore** is usually of **low grade**, less than 2% tin;
- the **quality of the ore is becoming** even **poorer** because the best veins have been used, and production is now little more than a third of what it was at its peak;
- Bolivia is a **landlocked country** (8.4), with no direct access to the coast. Export is by difficult rail connections, particularly to the Chilean ports of Antofagasta and Arica.

The tin miners work in appalling conditions. Most of the mines are primitive, and the miners suffer from silicosis, caused by breathing in dust in the mines. Their families live in monotonous barrack-like terraces in inhospitable mountain settlements (8.5). Methods of extracting and concentrating the ore are often by hand (8.6),

▲ 8.5 Mining settlement in the Bolivian Andes

▼ 8.6 Concentrating tin ore by hand, Bolivia

which makes the tin costly to produce. This means it is difficult to sell on the world's markets because:

(a) it has to **compete with low-cost tin**, more easily extracted by highly mechanised methods in accessible low-lying areas of Malaysia;

(b) it suffers from major **fluctuations in world prices**. These do not, of course, only affect the Bolivian economy. They also affect the well-being of the miners and their families. The miners take as much interest in world tin prices as financiers of the tin trade in the world's great commercial capitals. If asked what the price of tin is, most people in Britain would be unable to answer, though it is quoted daily in the newspapers. An illiterate Bolivian Indian may know the figure to within two decimal points. For in Bolivia a rise or fall of two points in the price of tin can mean the difference between eating and not eating. The North rarely considers this point of view.

Cooperation: international aid

Overseas programmes began in the 1940s, but since the 1960s these have slowed down. The Brandt Report suggests that each country in the North should put 0.7% of its gross national product (GNP) into overseas aid to the South by 1985. Table 8.2 shows that only the oil-rich states (which are technically in the South) gave more than this in 1983. Most countries in the North contribute far less than 0.7%. All in all, the world spends 25 times as much on defence weapons as it does on official development aid.

Three types of aid can be distinguished: official aid; voluntary aid; and commercial aid.

Official aid

This may be sent (in the form of money or goods) from individual governments direct to the countries in need of help. Or it may be channelled indirectly through international organisations. Among these are the following agencies of the United Nations (8.7):

- *Food and Agriculture Organisation* (FAO), with its headquarters in Rome;
- *World Bank*, headquarters in Washington and Paris;
- *United Nation Educational, Scientific and Cultural Organisation* (UNESCO), headquarters in Paris;
- *World Health Organisation* (WHO), headquarters in Geneva.

▲ 8.7 Headquarters of the United Nations, New York

Table 8.2 Official assistance to developing countries as percentage of GNP, 1983

Kuwait	3.5
Saudi Arabia	1.5
Average for all OPEC countries	0.77
Denmark/France/Netherlands/ Norway/Sweden	0.7
Other EEC countries, including UK	0.36
Austria/Finland/Switzerland	0.36
Australia/New Zealand/Japan/ Canada	0.36

Table 8.3 Countries with large debts

	$ Thousand million
Mexico (MI)	66.7
Brazil (MI)	58.0
Indonesia (LI)	21.7
Korea (MI)	21.5
India (LI)	21.3
Turkey (MI)	15.4
Egypt (MI)	15.2
Algeria (MI)	12.9

MI Middle-income developing country
LI Low-income developing country
(Source: *World Bank Report 1985*)

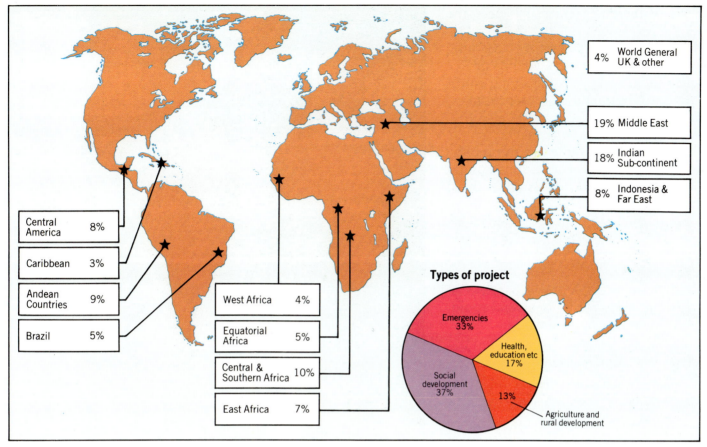

▲ 8.8 Oxfam: aid distribution, 1983–4

Voluntary aid

Large numbers of voluntary organisations promote overseas aid, and these have become increasingly important. They include, among others:

- *Band Aid*, the brain-child of Bob Geldof, which relies on funds raised by rock and pop musicians;
- *Centre for World Development Education*, to increase knowledge about the developing world;
- *Christian Aid*, the official development agency of the British Council of Churches;
- *Oxfam*, which raises large amounts of money for relief and development projects (3.15);
- *Population Concern*, which spreads population information and raises funds for family planning projects;
- *Save the Children Fund*, which raises relief and development funds for children's welfare.

Commercial aid

This is designed for economic support and not for social welfare. Over two-thirds of the loans made to developing countries are provided by commercial banks. But they charge high rates of interest. Some of these countries are greatly in debt, and can hardly afford even to repay the interest they owe on the loans, far less the loans themselves. In 1985, eight countries owed over $10 million (Table 8.3). One country, Mauritania (Sahel), had a greater debt than its GNP.

What is aid used for?

Where does overseas aid go, and what is it used for? 8.8 shows how one voluntary organisation, Oxfam, distributes its aid. It is used as follows:

- **Social development**, including projects in energy, industry, transport, water supply and sewage: 37%.
- **Agriculture and rural development**: 13%.
- **Health, education**, etc: 17%.
- **Emergencies**, such as drought or civil war: 33%.

One of the emergencies has been the recurring drought in the Sahel. Development projects involve working with small local groups, giving advice to help them improve their living conditions, farming methods, water supplies, health and hygiene.

Official organisations such as the World Bank also divide out the money they receive from contributions among various needs. Aid to Bangladesh in 1980/1, for example, was $334 million. More of this went on social development ($195 million) and agricultural and rural development ($58) than for direct welfare purposes.

It is not possible to separate out clearly the three forms of overseas aid, but in general it can be said that:

(a) *official international aid* concentrates on *large-scale development projects*;

(b) *voluntary aid* concentrates on *small-scale development, welfare and emergencies*;

(c) *commercial aid* is not really aid in the proper sense, since it takes the form of loans by banks on which interest has to be paid. The money borrowed may be used for internal development or other purposes. Unfortunately, large amounts of this money are spent on weapons used for fighting in civil wars, against guerrillas, or even in external wars.

Case study: distress in Ethiopia

As 8.9 shows, the 'Horn of Africa' is largely made up of two countries, Ethiopia and Somalia. These have been at war for some time over the disputed Ogaden area on their borders. There has also been civil war in Ethiopia. Large areas of Tigre and Eritrea (8.9) are not under government control. These conflicts have created one of the world's most distressed areas. It has been hit by the natural hazard of drought and by these human conflicts.

The plight of Ethiopia's refugees in the famine-stricken areas (8.10) so disturbed the pop singer, Bob Geldof, that he decided to raise money through the sales of a Christmas 1984 record 'Band

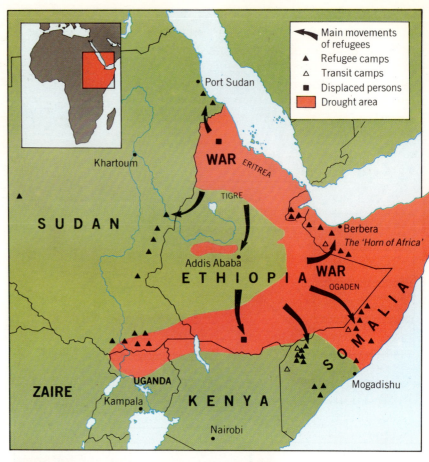

▲ 8.9 Distress in the Horn of Africa

◀ 8.10 Starvation in Ethiopia

▼ 8.11 Live Aid concert, July 1985

Aid' made by a large group of well-known pop singers. This was so successful that he went on to form a relief organisation named Band Aid which raised money through various projects including a huge Live Aid concert at Wembley, London, in July 1985 (8.11). As the newspaper extract (8.12) shows, Band Aid relief has supplemented that of governments and organisations such as Oxfam.

One of the great problems faced by relief organisations is getting the food to the refugees in war-torn and inaccessible areas, as described in the following account.

'Looking through the window of the plane, the passenger notices the deep ravines and gorges that criss-cross the landscape and the steep gorges and mountains that divide the high plateau. He or she will not see a single road, not one electric pylon, no stretch of railway, nothing that vaguely resembles any modern development... How on earth can anyone live on such inaccessible ledges, I found myself wondering? They are utterly cut off from the facilities of the modern world.'

Geldof aid gets to famine areas other agencies cannot reach

by David Blundy
Addis Ababa

BOB GELDOF and Kevin Jenden, the director of Band Aid, reached Ethiopia on the last leg of their trip across the Sahel region of Africa on Friday night. As the plane flew at 37,000 feet near Asmara in northern Ethiopia, tracer bullets could be seen flashing in the mountains, stark evidence of the Ethiopean army's offensive against the Eritrean rebels.

• • •

Across Africa there was evidence of how Band Aid money, a tiny amount compared to the billions of dollars of aid pumped into Africa, had been spent and how it had helped.

Egil Hagen, the head of Unicef emergency operations in Sudan, said that without the Band Aid contributions hundreds of people would have died. "Without their initiative we couldn't have started the fast-moving distribution of medical supplies," he said. "When cholera broke out in eastern Sudan in June we had to intervene quickly. Band Aid sent 3m doses of antibiotics and intravenous fluid and we had them into the camps within days." In one camp, Wad Sharifi, there were 1,733 cases of cholera. There were 32 deaths and these would have turned into hundreds if the medicine had not arrived quickly.

In a shanty town in Port Sudan called the Devil's Horn, which is built on a rubbish dump and houses 60,000 people, Band Aid had funded a school and a clinic. It has taken food to the isolated tribes in the Red Sea hills. It is the only agency flying supplies into Boonja, in rebel-heid southern Sudan. It is one of the few funding shipments of food and medicine into the rebel areas of Ethiopia and into Wollo, in central Ethiopia.

▲ 8.12 (*The Sunday Times*, 20 October 1985)

◀ 8.13 UNICEF convoy in the Sahel

Lorries, such as the UNICEF convoy in 8.13, struggle to get through the sandy eroded terrain. Sometimes communications break down altogether, and food is left to rot at the ports (8.14).

The huge international Ethiopian relief effort of 1985 has, however, had some success, and food has got through by land and air to the refugee camps (8.15). After the years of drought the summer rains in 1985 were better than for some years, and crops were planted. But the problems of Ethiopia and the countries of the Sahel remain the most distressing on earth.

◀ 8.14 Relief food rotting at a port

▶ 8.15 Red Cross aid at an Ethiopian refugee camp

Index

agriculture *see* farming

Arab world (Moslem/Islam)
    education of girls   28
    Islamic faith   41, 42
    oil-rich states   20, 21, 60
capitalist world (Occidental/Western)
    high-income countries   21
    NATO   43
    political differences with communism   43, 44
    Westernised consumer society   56
climatic divisions
    equatorial   54
    hot desert   4, 5, 6, 33
    monsoon   15, 23
    mountain   4, 6
    savanna (Sahel)   33
    tropical marine   37
colonialism
    colonisation (European settlers)   11, 42, 48, 49
    New Commonwealth countries   11
    slave trade   11, 12
communication barriers
    Berlin Wall   45
    high relief   59, 63
communist world
    Berlin Wall   45
    developed world   19, 20
    high-income countries   21
    political differences with capitalism   43, 44
    spread of   43, 44, 45
    Warsaw Pact   43
    Vietnam War   12
conservation
    forests   53, 54, 55
    natural resources   51, 52, 53, 54, 55, 56
    water supplies   26, 52

deserts
    desertification   33
    drought   29, 33, 34, 63
    irrigation   23
    landscape   4, 5
developed countries
    characteristics   19, 20, 24
    high-income countries   21, 57
    slow population growth   8
developing countries
    characteristics   19, 20
    educational provision   17, 20
    famine   25
    low-income countries   19, 20, 21, 22, 24, 57

medical provision   20, 24
middle-income countries   19, 20, 21, 22, 24, 57
rapid population growth   7, 8, 9, 10
urbanisation   13
economic factors
    capital investment   40
    competition   58, 60
    economic aid   *see* international (overseas) aid
    low wages   50
    multiplier effect   40
    tariffs   58
    world prices   58, 59, 60
    world recession   40
educational provision
    correspondence courses   28
    developing countries   20, 28
    girls' education   28
    illiteracy   20
    international (overseas) aid   28
employment
    casual workers (seasonal employment)   14, 17, 40, 48
    tourism   40
    unemployment   11, 17, 40
environmental perception
    city environments   18, 40
    'hostile' environments   6

farming
    collective farming   43–4
    contour ploughing   51
    crop spraying   23
    crop yields   23
    drainage   23
    fertilisers   23
    Green Revolution   23
    irrigation   23
    labour-intensive farming   22
    land reclamation   23
    plantation crops   31, 39, 49, 58
    subsistence farming   19, 22, 23
    terracing   4, 5, 22, 23, 31, 51, 55
    windbreaks   51, 62
food
    diet   19, 24, 25, 26
    malnutrition   25, 50
    staple foods   19
    supplies of (supplementary feeding)   22, 23, 25, 40
forests
    afforestation (reafforestation)   51, 55
    building materials   55
    deforestation   51, 53, 54, 55, 56

fuel   55
secondary forest   55
timber products   53, 54, 58
gross national product (GNP)
    high-income countries   21, 60
    low-income countries   21
    middle-income countries   21
health (disease)
    dietary deficiency diseases   25, 50
    economic costs of disease   26
    endemic diseases   26
    famine   25, 34, 45, 63
    infantile mortality   20, 24, 50
    infectious (airborne) disease   26, 48
    intestinal diseases   26
    life expectancy   24
    malnutrition   25, 50
    medical services/supplies   20, 24, 27, 61, 63
    primary health care   27
    sanitation (safe water supply)   15, 17, 27
    silicosis   59
    vaccines   27
    vector-borne diseases   26
human conflict
    cultural differences   41
    ethnic (racial) differences   41, 46, 47, 48, 49, 50
    language differences   41, 42, 43
    political differences   41, 43, 44, 45
    religious differences   41, 42

insect pests
    locusts   29, 34, 35
    mosquitoes   34
    pest control   35
    plagues   29, 35
    tsetse flies   34, 35
interdependence
    Brandt Report   57, 60
    See also international (overseas) aid
international (overseas) aid
    Band Aid   61, 62, 63
    Centre for World Development Education   61
    Christian Aid   61
    commercial (economic) aid   60, 61, 62
    educational provision   28, 61
    Food and Agricultural Organisation (FAO)   60
    official organisations   25, 60, 62
    Oxfam   25, 61